Table of Contents

The Well-Presented Manuscript

Just What You Need to Know to Make Your Fiction Look Professional

by Mike Reeves-McMillan

Revised and expanded fourth edition 2025.

A C-Side Media production.

Cover by Matt Davis of Rock and Hill Studio.

If you're reading this book, you're probably a writer yourself, so I don't need to go into a long spiel about piracy and compensating the author, do I? Good.

Dedicated to my favourite teacher, the late Dr. Scott Allen, who nurtured my love of language through his entertaining and memorable lectures.

The aardvarks are for him.

Introduction

More than 90% of what gets submitted to editors—both fiction magazine editors and publishing house editors—is rejected as soon as a reader sees it, often because it doesn't meet basic standards of competence in presentation and language use. This book gives you a guide to meeting those standards.

Meeting them will help with self-publishing too, since discerning readers also reject books that don't meet them. A review, or, even worse, multiple reviews that mention basic errors in your prose can do a lot of harm to your sales.

You may even be missing out on sales because you're making simple mistakes in your blurb, and putting people off before they read a word of your book. I can't count how many books I've dismissed sight unseen because an error in the blurb suggested that the book would contain many more distracting errors. A blurb is a job interview. It pays to dress nicely.

Beyond just getting past the gatekeepers (including readers and reviewers), developing the skill of communicating clearly with standard punctuation, grammar and usage will help you become a better writer. A musician plays notes; a great musician knows why those notes, in that relationship, work together, and what effect that will have on the audience, because a great musician thinks about the notes, and plays only the ones he or she means to play. For us as writers, words are our notes.

Also, if you're offering a product for sale, I think it's reasonable to expect a basic standard of professionalism in its preparation. The author should put in the work to make things easier for the reader, rather than leaving the reader working hard to understand what they mean.

Many authors don't know how to do that, though, which is why I wrote this book. They aren't lazy or stupid; they've just never been taught. Berating them for not knowing something that nobody ever told them is not helpful.

I review a lot of books—more than a hundred in a year, sometimes—and I see the same easily corrected errors over and over. In fact, I have a habit of marking the errors I see as I'm reading, and since I do this on my Kindle, I have a record. Since I first got a Kindle in late 2011, I've noted more than 25,000 errors in over a thousand books, most of them published (some I read before publication in order to review them), a good many of them traditionally published. I worked it out once at more than two dozen errors per book, on average, which I've noticed on a casual read-through, ranging from one or two or even zero errors at one end of the quality spectrum to well over 100 at the other. I found about 400 errors in one particularly awful book (before its publication, but not very long before). And as part of writing this book, I've analysed these errors to figure out which basic problems are most common. Many of the examples I'll give come directly from those books, with character names and other identifying details anonymized; I'm not setting out to name and shame the authors, just because nobody ever taught them a rule. I do name one or two very prominent authors who should know better, and whose reputation is not going to be dented by my criticism, and also one or two authors who do things particularly well.

I've generally not given examples that I've seen outside published or soon-to-be-published fiction, unless they are in what should be a professional context (a website with some prestige, for example), and illustrate an issue I've also seen in fiction. If I started listing errors I've seen in other people's book reviews or, even worse, on social media or in comment sections, I'd never finish. Besides, those aren't making any claim, even implicitly, to be professional writing.

A lot of available guides that are otherwise useful are either in blog format, providing somewhat scattershot advice with no overarching plan, or else are too comprehensive, giving advice on every little thing—including things that people rarely get wrong or even use—so that you have to sift through it to find what's relevant to your needs. I aim to hit the Goldilocks zone between the two.

There are several good grammar sites around, most notably Grammar Girl (http://www.quickanddirtytips.com/grammar-girl), but they do tend to focus on theory and get deep into the detail, and they're for a wide audience, not just writers of fiction. The famous *Strunk & White* is, I'm afraid, overcomplicated, outdated, and doesn't always follow its own (sometimes bad) advice. Other guides are mainly oriented towards business or academic writing. This guide is written by a fiction writer—one who's also a former book editor and technical writer, and a current book reviewer and beta reader—as a practical tool for other fiction writers.

I'd say that, out of the authors whose books are appealing enough for me to actually pick up and try to read, at least 70% make at least one of the types of errors I cover here (and I filter out a lot of books that are probably worse, based on the blurb, so the overall percentage is likely to be higher). If you can eliminate them, that will make your manuscript cleaner than most.

Note that this book isn't about writing the actual story, which is another set of skills above and beyond these. It's about meeting the basic standards that will get your story read in the first place.

The aim is to provide just enough information to help you look competent, so I won't go into the finer details in some cases. For example, there are some arcane comma rules that are really only known or understood by advanced editors and grammarians, and if you don't observe them, nobody but a serious pedant will dock you points. I'll point to places where you can find details about those rules if you want—if your comma usage is generally good already, knowing these rules will make it excellent—but if you struggle with the basics of commas, you don't need to confuse yourself with these more advanced rules.

Does every editor care about these things? No—as poorly-edited books from major publishing houses demonstrate—but most will. Does every reader? Absolutely not—as five-star reviews for books that are full of errors demonstrate—but some will, and even people who rate such a book highly can sometimes get a vague sense of something wrong with it. I reviewed a book, for example (the 400-errors one) where another reviewer remarked that she found the book confusing at times, but blamed herself. It was not her fault; the author had written multiple sentences that made no grammatical or logical sense, spelled words incorrectly or used entirely the wrong word for what she meant (sometimes a word that was so wrong I couldn't even figure out which word she'd intended).

If you want to communicate "I am basically professional," and if you want people who read your writing not to be distracted or confused by simple language mistakes so they can concentrate on your story, this book is here to help you achieve that standard.

I use grammatical terminology throughout, not in an attempt to make your eyes glaze over, but for two practical reasons. Firstly, having a term for something helps me to talk about it clearly, and secondly, if you want to look up more information on a rule, it helps to know the formal name for it. Don't worry about learning the terminology; there isn't going to be an exam. Use it if it helps, ignore it if it doesn't help.

There's a great deal more to English grammar than what I present here, and some of it gets horribly complicated. I have just stuck to what I believe will be helpful to fiction writers in avoiding common errors. A real grammar expert, which I am not, would say I oversimplify in places, but since I'm not setting out to train academic grammarians, I'm comfortable with that.

Very few places appear to be teaching these skills, so it's no wonder so few authors have them. Certainly, my degree in English language and literature didn't cover basic writing mechanics, and based on the state of a number of books I've read by people who have creative writing degrees, creative writing courses don't either. I've even seen several books written by high school English teachers who make very basic errors, which suggests three things to me: firstly, this material isn't in the curriculum, or they'd know it; secondly, if students are making the same errors, the teachers don't know enough to correct them; and thirdly, they're modelling incorrect practice to their students. It's therefore not surprising that I see these errors cropping up over and over in published fiction. Nobody ever taught the authors how to do it correctly.

I've used the word "correctly" there, and that needs some discussion. Like most people with formal education in the subtleties of the English language, I am more what is called a "descriptivist" than a "prescriptivist". A descriptivist describes how language is actually used, and a prescriptivist attempts to prescribe (lay down the law about) how it *should* be used, sometimes making up rules that few people actually follow. Descriptivists acknowledge that language changes as usage changes.

However, even a descriptivist can regard some usages as mistakes, such as when two similar words are confused, or when the normal punctuation conventions that most people observe are not followed. Being a descriptivist doesn't mean that any usage at all is considered correct usage. Only usage that is widespread and general is considered correct usage. What I am setting out to teach you in this book, then, are the widespread, general standards of English usage.

Also, if usage determines correctness, I want to do all I can to encourage usage that makes sense, that preserves the distinctions between similar words so that our vocabulary remains rich and flexible, and that is easy for readers to follow.

At the same time, I don't want to give you a long list of small niggling distinctions that nobody except a professional nitpicker cares about, including made-up rules like "a preposition is something you shouldn't end a sentence with," which has never been actual English usage.

I've tried, instead, to target the mistakes that I believe make a difference to meaning, clarity, and the experience of the reader. That's not to say that some of your readers won't get all sniffy if you break one of the made-up rules (or if they think you have), but there are so many of those theoretical rules, and so many people have been half-educated in them, that there's probably no avoiding that problem if your audience includes such people (unless you write such uptight prose that most ordinary people will wonder what your problem is). Though, as I discuss further in the Lay vs Lie section, sometimes you do have to cater to your audience's expectations of what correct usage is *for the context you're writing about*, even if that means doing something that you wouldn't usually do if you were writing in your own voice.

Along the way, I will occasionally be opinionated. I'm sure you can deal with that.

What's Changed in the Fourth Edition

The last two editions of this book opened with the five most common errors. I've now completely restructured it to refer to the ten most common *types* of errors:

1. **Vocabulary.** I now provide almost 200 entries on pairs, trios, or single words that I've seen confused with each other or used incorrectly in published fiction, and explain how to use them.
2. **Apostrophe usage.** Two simple rules will enable you to get the apostrophe in the right place every time.
3. **Narrative tense.** How to stop jerking your readers around in time so they have a smooth reading experience. Revised and expanded.
4. **Commas of identity** (vocative and appositive commas). How to fix one of the easiest ways to spot amateurish writing.
5. **Commas of sequence** (coordinate commas and lists). How to avoid an error that even some good writers still make. Revised and expanded.
6. **Commas of grammatical structure** (phrasal commas). How to know where—and where not—to put a comma, without having to guess.
7. **Capitalization, hyphenation and other punctuation marks.** Every error I've seen (and there are a lot of them), described and corrected.
8. **Dialog punctuation.** A persistent problem for a minority of writers, with a few easy rules.
9. **Clarity of reference** (number agreement, pronoun errors,

dangling modifiers). Make sure your readers understand exactly what you're talking about without having to stop and work it out. Revised and expanded.

10. **Research and knowledge**. Common slip-ups that are easily corrected. Revised and expanded, including an extensive guide to differences between British and American English for authors who speak one, but whose characters speak the other.

I end with an extended section on the parts of speech: noun, pronoun, subject, object, verb, adjective, adverb, preposition, etc. I don't put it up front, because some people won't need it and others will find it daunting; instead, I refer to it when necessary. In fact, I constantly refer back and forth between the two parts: the things people get wrong and the basics of language.

The 2025 edition is 20% longer than the 2022 edition, which itself was 40% longer than the 2020 edition, but I have cut some material as well as adding. Some of it is duplication that I've now merged and trimmed down in the new, more logical structure. The rest is material that I didn't think was particularly relevant or valuable, because you can get it elsewhere and it isn't what the book is mainly about—namely the section on how to submit short stories to editors. That was part of my initial vision for the book, but my focus has shifted and narrowed to explaining the common errors I see in published fiction and how to avoid making them.

When I read nonfiction books, I sometimes reflect that they would be improved by a clearer vision for what they're setting out to achieve and a better structure that served that purpose. I hope that this revised edition brings this book closer to that ideal.

Apologies to anyone who bought one of the previous editions, has updated to this one, and now finds that everything is in a different place and you have to search for it. I think the improvement justifies the change.

Conventions

Throughout the book, wherever I give an example, unless I embed it in the sentence describing it, it will be indented from the left margin. If the example is of something that's incorrect, it will be marked with a ~~strikethrough~~, so you're left in no doubt that you shouldn't do it.

I've marked many of the errors based on how common they are, as follows:

**** Extremely common. Even some people who make few errors sometimes make this one.

*** Common. I see this error all the time.

** Uncommon. I see this error occasionally.

* Rare. I've only seen this error once or twice.

You might wonder why I bother to even mention the rare errors. There are two reasons.

First, if one person has made the error there are probably others.

Second, rare errors, by definition, are the ones where most people know the rule. This means that the one- and two-star errors are ones that most readers will notice, so it's especially important not to make them. If you make a four-star error, many editors won't even notice (though some definitely will).

Three-star errors—the ones that many people make, but not the people who really know what they're doing—are probably the most important to focus on, though. There's a high likelihood that you're making them, and getting them right will lift you above the crowd.

Style and Voice

In order to explain the main purpose of this book, I need to talk about style and voice.

Style is about the choices you make between valid alternatives. For example, do you use parentheses, dashes, or commas to set off a clause that "interrupts" the main sentence, or do you not put such clauses in at all? All of these are valid choices, and if you make one particular choice consistently, it becomes part of your style.

Voice is largely, but not completely, made up of the sum of all your style choices. It also takes in point of view, word choice, and a few less definable qualities. This is what tells us that we are reading Ursula K. Le Guin rather than Neil Gaiman, however similar their writing might be in some ways.

Voice is also something that belongs to characters, as well as authors, and one of the skills that raises authors above mediocrity is the ability to give their characters distinctive voices. Again, point of view, the things they notice and talk about, has a lot to do with it, but so do stylistic choices. I sometimes make my characters sound less like me by having them choose a word which wasn't the one I first thought of.

George Orwell, in a famous essay, spoke about language which, like clear glass, was there for people to look through, and other kinds of language which were like stained glass: designed to be looked at. In fact, there's a spectrum of style, which Jeff Vandermeer sums up well in *Wonderbook*. (I recommend that book, by the way, which is about all the writing skills that I *don't* cover here: how to find ideas and develop them into stories. You'll find full details in the Other Resources section at the back of this book.)

Vandermeer mentions four levels of style, which, as I'm sure he'd be the first to acknowledge, are points on a spectrum rather than distinct quantum steps.

Minimal or stark style has hardly any detail or description, leaving a lot to the reader's imagination. Done badly, it's dull and unengaging, emotionally distant and ploddingly literal. Done well, it has the beauty of simplicity and purity.

Invisible or "normal" style aims to disappear, like Orwell's clear glass window. It's the most common style of writing, particularly for commercial fiction. Although it doesn't sound the way people actually talk, because we're used to fictional conventions we think of it as sounding like the voices of real, ordinary people. Done badly, it's mediocre, bland and lacklustre. Done well, it lets the reader focus on the story.

Muscular or conspicuous style uses more sensory detail, more metaphors, and more complex sentences than ordinary people tend to in real life. It draws a little attention to itself. Done badly, it seems too clever and gets in the way of the story. Done well, it feels rich and vivid.

Lush or ornate style draws a lot of attention to itself, like a beautiful woman dancing in a sequined dress. Extended metaphors, long sentences, passages of pure description, language tricks borrowed from poetry, unusual word choices and a layering of detail give an overall richness to the prose. Done badly, it's like wading through treacle, and produces impatience in the reader who just wants to know what happened next. Done well, it's glorious, a work of high art.

The commonest style, and the one that's easiest to read and easiest to write, is "invisible" style. My advice in this book is aimed at helping you to write invisibly, because if you use the basic tools of language correctly, nobody will notice that you're using them. Using them badly draws attention to your writing, for all the wrong reasons. It's like you're a cabinetmaker, and you've left tool marks on all your surfaces and your joints don't fit well. People will notice that you're incompetent with your tools, rather than noticing the piece of furniture and forgetting that it was made with tools at all.

Myself, I wouldn't advise attempting anything other than invisible style until you can write invisible style competently and smoothly. I see far too many people trying to write in a lush style like authors they admire (most commonly Jack Vance, Lord Dunsany or H.P. Lovecraft) without the basic grasp of language and style that those authors possessed. In particular, if your vocabulary isn't as large as you think it is (and most people's isn't), you'll embarrass yourself by using fancy words that you don't really know the meaning of. I see this all the time in books I review. If you're going to use a fancy word, look it up and make sure it means what you think it means.

The more you depart from normal or invisible style, the more obvious any mistakes will be, because the other styles deliberately call attention to your use of language. If you attempt a lush style, in particular, without understanding exactly what you're doing, it will fail, and fail horribly. A lot of readers don't like lush style much even when it's done well (I'm one of them), and seeing it done badly is agonising.

The time to let your prose draw attention to itself by dancing is *after* you're confident that it won't draw attention to itself by falling flat on its face.

By the way, if you want to read a wonderful (though tragic and heartwrenching) example of the use of changes in style and voice to convey a character's experience of the world, find a copy of Daniel Keyes' *Flowers for Algernon*—either the original short story, or the novel that he later expanded it into. It's the journal of an intellectually disabled man who gets an experimental treatment that increases his intelligence to well above average, and what the author does with language is brilliant. The impact of the story would be much less without it.

It's also a great example of knowing when to break the rules. All rules—even the ones for correct punctuation—can be broken to create a deliberate effect (such as conveying the writing of a semi-literate, intellectually disabled man). Some people will tell you not to worry about the rules, that telling a good story is the important thing. Telling a good story is extremely important, but another important thing is to know the rules, and know the effect that you'll get from following them, and the effect that you'll get from not following them, and choose which effect you want—rather than accidentally create the effect of looking unprofessional.

Accordingly, every piece of advice in this book (and any other book about writing) should be understood to have a silent qualifier: "Follow the rule, unless breaking the rule achieves the exact effect you want."

Section 1: The Ten Most Common Types of Errors

Chapter 1: Vocabulary

"You keep using that word. I don't think it means what you think it means."

– Inigo Montoya in William Goldman's *The Princess Bride.*

Errors of vocabulary are among the most common errors I see. There are a couple of reasons for that.

One is that English has such a huge number of words, more than almost any other language; the Oxford English Dictionary lists around 170,000 words in current use, though many of these, of course, are restricted to specific areas of expertise. Most English-speaking people have a passive vocabulary (words they understand) of around 40,000 and an active vocabulary (words they use themselves) about half that. But if their writing is any guide, a lot of people have a much smaller vocabulary than they think they do, and are prone to confusing words that look or sound similar.

The other reason that I see so many vocabulary errors is that spellcheck won't catch them. If you write a word that isn't the word you mean, but is in your spellcheck dictionary, you won't be alerted to it. Only alertness and a keen, knowledgeable eye will pick them up. Or, if you're reading on an e-reader, you can highlight any word you're the least bit unsure about, and it will give you the definition. Google Docs will do the same, if you highlight the word, right-click and choose "Define" from the context menu, and newer versions of MS Word have a similar function (called "search" in the context menu). I believe the popular writing software Scrivener also provides this functionality.

Some tools (including Google Docs) will alert you to possible vocabulary errors with a visual cue, though their suggestions should always be checked, because they're sometimes wrong too.

The following list is based on errors I've seen myself in published or soon-to-be-published fiction. Reviewers have told me that they found it one of the most useful parts of the book, and that's one of the two reasons I'm now putting it first, the other reason being that vocabulary errors are among the most common errors I see.

Terminology: A *homonym* is a word that sounds like another word but means something different. Technically, it's a word that sounds exactly like another, but I've included some examples where the word is sometimes confused with one that sounds approximately like it, or that only sounds like it in some accents.

Homonym errors are *extremely* common. Some are more common than others, of course, and as with other errors in the book, I've marked these with more asterisks (*) so you can review them.

For some reason, I usually see a lot of homonym errors in books set before World War I, whether they're steampunk, gaslight fantasy, Regency romance or historical. I think people who write those books try for a more formal and verbose vocabulary than they usually use, to try to capture the feel of the writing from that period, and because it's not their usual vocabulary they end up making more mistakes with it. After all, in modern life we have a lot of vocabulary for things that didn't exist a hundred years ago, and some of that has inevitably pushed out older words which are now less used and so less familiar.

Superhero novels and litRPG are also prone to homonym errors, but they're prone to more errors in general; for some reason, those genres attract authors who have a particularly loose grasp on basic writing tools.

General note: The words for which I have given a literal definition below are sometimes used metaphorically. This doesn't change the fact that you should use the right spelling for the metaphor you intend.

Easily Confused Words

---

* ABBOT/ABBOTT

An **abbot** is in charge of an abbey.

Abbott, with two Ts, is a surname. (Compare marshal/Marshall, clerk/Clark, tailor/Taylor, gardener/Gardner, other surnames that originated in occupations that have since diverged from the surname in spelling.)

*ADAPT/ADOPT

adapt means to change in order to meet changing circumstances.

adopt means to take on (a practice, etc.).

A well-known couple who write about the business of writing consistently use the phrase "early adapters" when they mean "early adopters". As far as I know, they're not being deliberately clever; they just have the phrase wrong.

*ADIEU/ADO

adieu is a French word meaning "goodbye".

ado means unnecessary delay, drama, or messing about. It is the word to use in the expression "without further ado" and in the title of Shakespeare's play *Much Ado About Nothing*. Do not substitute "adieu" into this expression.

**ADMISSION/ADMITTANCE

admission is what you're charged to get into a place, or a confession that you've done something.

admittance is being allowed to enter somewhere, usually in the phrase "no admittance".

***ADVANCE/ADVANCED

If you mean "beforehand," use **advance** (as in the phrase "in advance"; also "advance notice," "Advance Reader Copy").

If you mean "sophisticated," use **advanced**.

*ADVERSE/AVERSE

Effects are **adverse** (negative).

People are **averse** (disinclined) to do things.

****AFFECT/EFFECT

This is an especially confusing pair.

affect is usually a verb: Raising interest rates will affect how many people borrow money.

effect is usually a noun: The effect of raising interest rates is that fewer people borrow money.

However, there is a noun "affect" (pronounced with the emphasis on the first syllable instead of the second, AF-fect) which is used in psychology to mean "the ability to feel things": He suffered from flat affect.

And there is a verb "effect" meaning "to bring about", usually applied to change: The new government plans to effect an immediate change in interest rates.

The safest thing with this pair is to check every time until you get it right consistently.

**AFFIX/FIX

To **affix** means to attach something to something else: He affixed the bar code to the shelf. It is usually literal and physical.

To **fix** can mean the same thing, or it can be used metaphorically for fixing one's attention, or eyes, on an object, for example, in which case "affix" is not the word to use.

Fix can also mean "repair," but *affix* does not.

*AFTERWARD/AFTERWORD

afterward means "subsequently".

An **afterword** is a note from the author at the end of a book. At the beginning of the book, it's a **foreword**.

***AID/AIDE

aid means assistance: I came to his aid. This is the word you use in "first aid".

An **aide** is someone who assists: Her aide handed her the relevant folder.

**ALIGHT/LIGHT

A bird can **alight** on a branch (meaning land).

A lantern or a fire can be referred to as **alight** (meaning it's been lit).

But you cannot ~~alight a fire~~. You **light** a fire.

**ALLOW/LET

These words are synonyms, but there is a subtle difference of usage. You **let** someone do something, but you **allow** someone *to* do something. The "to" is required.

**ALLUDE/ELUDE

allude means to refer: He alluded to the Noodle Incident.

elude means to escape: He eluded his pursuers.

**ALLUSIVE/ELUSIVE/ILLUSIVE

allusive means making use of allusion (that is, indirect references to things).

elusive means hard to catch.

illusive is an old-fashioned word meaning illusionary, not real.

**ALTAR/ALTER

An **altar** is a focus for worship, usually in a church or temple.

To **alter** something is to change it.

*ANCESTOR/DESCENDANT

Your **ancestors** are your parents, grandparents, and so on up your family tree into the past. You are descended from them, but they are your ancestors.

Your **descendants** are your children, grandchildren, and so on down your family tree into the future.

Besides seeing these two confused, I've also seen the word "~~ascendant~~" used as the opposite of "descendant". The author meant "ancestor".

****ANY MORE/ANYMORE

any more means "a further quantity": He didn't want any more beer. (He had already had enough beer.)

anymore always refers to time, when something has changed from how it used to be: He didn't like beer anymore. (He used to like beer, but now he didn't.)

British English doesn't tend to make the distinction, and uses "any more" for both, but if you are writing American English, use "anymore" to refer to time and "any more" to refer to quantity.

*APPRAISE/APPRISE

When you **appraise** an object, you're estimating its value, and you're probably an expert.

You **apprise** someone of an important piece of information.

**ASCRIBE/SUBSCRIBE

You **ascribe** a quality to someone or something, meaning that you believe that it has that quality.

You **subscribe** to a belief or philosophy.

*AUGHT/NAUGHT

aught is an old-fashioned word for "anything".

naught is an old-fashioned word for "nothing".

*AWARD/REWARD

The usage of these two words is subtly different. You **award** something *to* a person; you **reward** a person *with* something. You do not ~~reward them something~~. You can, however, award them with something. There's a subtle distinction in connotation as well; an award usually implies a prize, which often has primarily symbolic value and gives status (though it can carry a cash value with it too), while a reward implies something of (usually) monetary value that has been earned by one's actions.

****BACKWARD/BACKWARDS**

(British and Commonwealth English only; American English does not make this distinction, usually using "backward" for both.)

A **backward** society is not advanced.

A **backwards** society would be one in which things were wrong way round, like Bizarro World or Wonderland.

****BASE/BASS**

The **base** of something is the bottom of it.

bass (pronounced the same) is the lowest part of music.

***BATED/BAITED**

You wait for something with **bated** breath (originally "abated," meaning you've stopped breathing until it happens).

A fishhook is **baited**.

*****BEAR/BARE**

To **bear** something means to carry it. Think of a bear (the animal) carrying something, if it helps.

To **bare** something means to reveal it, to strip off its covering. If you talk about "~~the right to bare arms~~" you are referring to being allowed to wear sleeveless shirts.

*BEDCLOTHES/NIGHTCLOTHES

Your **bedclothes** are not the clothes you wear to bed; they are sheets and blankets. The clothes you wear to bed are **nightclothes**.

**BEHALF/BEHEST/PART

If I do something on someone's **behalf**, I am doing it for their benefit or in place of them: I spoke on his behalf.

If I do it at their **behest**, I am doing it because they asked me to.

If I mean "as for him," the expression is "on his **part**" (not ~~behalf~~).

*BEHEST/BEQUEATH/BEQUEST

If someone **bequeaths** something to you (that is, they leave it to you in their will), it is a **bequest**. There is no such word as ~~bequeathment~~.

You do something at someone's **behest** if you do it because they asked or told you to.

***BELIE/BETRAY

His open, honest face **belied** his devious nature. (It gave an impression that was the opposite of the truth.)

Her worried glance **betrayed** her concern. (It gave the truth away.)

As a general observation, add the "be-" prefix with care. It often changes the meaning of the root word. Don't use it simply to give an "old-timey" feel to language without understanding the meaning of the resulting word. "Bespeak" doesn't mean the same as "speak," for example. It means "to order".

**BERTH/BIRTH

A **berth** is somewhere you tie up a boat. It's also used in the expression "to give someone/something a wide berth," meaning to steer well clear of them.

A **birth** is the process of being born.

****BOARDER/BORDER**

A **boarder** is someone who either pays you money to live in your house, or is trying to force their way onto your ship.

A **border** is a line between two areas, such as two countries.

*****BORN/BORNE**

born refers to the process of birth: Macbeth could not be killed by one of woman born.

borne is the past tense of bear (carry): The coffin was borne on their shoulders.

Slightly confusingly, you can say "She has borne a child," meaning she carried the child within her and then gave birth to it.

*****BOTH/EACH**

See discussion of Both and Each in the Clarity of Reference chapter. Briefly, though: **both** means they're sharing, **each** means they're not. If you give something to two people, for example, saying you give it to both of them means that it's one thing shared between the two, but giving it to each of them means they got two things, one per person.

***BOW/BOUGH**

The spelling **bow** is used by several words with two different pronunciations, one of which is shared with the word spelled **bough**.

A **bow** (rhyming with "grow") can be tied on a package or used to launch an arrow or play a violin. It's also a verb meaning to bend like the arrow-launcher does.

A **bow** (rhyming with "how") is the action of bending at the waist, and it is also a verb in this meaning. It's the front of a ship, too.

A **bough** (rhyming with "how") is the limb of a tree.

***BRAKE/BREAK

break means to smash: I'm going to break your face!

brake means to slow down: He braked the car. He did so using its brakes.

****BREACH/BREECH

A **breech** is the back end of something (like a gun): The cartridge jammed in the breech. It's also used in "breeches," meaning trousers, which go on your back end.

A **breach** is a break, usually one that lets something through: The enemy poured in through the breach in the wall.

***BREATH/BREATHE

A **breath** is air you take into your lungs. It is a noun.

To **breathe** is to take air into your lungs. It is a verb.

Compare sheath (noun) and sheathe (verb).

*BRIEF/DEBRIEF

You are **briefed** before a mission and **debriefed** after it.

****BROACH/BROOCH

broach is a verb meaning to break open: He broached the cask.

A **brooch** is a decorative piece of jewellery, usually pinned to the clothing on a person's torso.

****CANON/CANNON

A **canon** is a group of creative or religious works (or a functionary in a cathedral, or a kind of musical piece, or official features of a fictional setting).

A **cannon** is a large artillery weapon.

*CANTER/CANTOR

A **canter** is a gait of a horse between a trot and a gallop.

A **cantor** leads singing in some religious traditions.

**CANVAS/CANVASS

canvas is a kind of cloth, used for sails and paintings.

To **canvass** is to conduct a poll or ask for votes.

**CAPITAL/CAPITOL

A **capital** is the main city of a country or state.

A **capitol** is, in the USA, the building in which the legislature meets. (Yes, the Hunger Games got it wrong.)

**CENSER/CENSOR/CENSURE

A **censer** holds incense: The priest waved the censer over the couple before pronouncing them married.

A **censor** is a person who works for the government and decides what may or may not be published: The chief censor has rated this movie PG. It is also a verb, meaning to perform the job of a censor.

censure means disapproval specifically expressed, often officially: The committee moved to censure him for his actions.

**CHAFFING/CHAFING

chaffing refers to friendly mockery: We were chaffing him about his new girlfriend.

chafing refers to friction against the skin: His shorts were chafing him.

***CHORD/CORD

A **chord** is a number of musical notes played simultaneously, with specific intervals between them.

A **cord** is something between thick string and thin rope.

Vocal cords are in your throat; vocal chords are sung by a choir.

**CLAMBER/CLAMOR

To **clamber** means to climb with difficulty.

To **clamor** means to make a loud, probably demanding noise.

**COMPRISE/COMPOSE

This one is the focus of some controversy. The word **comprise** means "is composed of," so some people argue that the expression "is comprised of" is incorrect and should be replaced by "is composed of," "consists of" or simply "comprises". However, "is comprised of" is accepted by several major dictionaries as correct usage, and has appeared in high-status publications since the early 18th century. As usual, usage trumps logic.

However, it is still regarded as incorrect to say "~~comprises of~~". Say either "is comprised of" or "comprises".

***COMPLEMENT/COMPLIMENT

complement means to go well together: The curtains complemented the carpet.

compliment means to say something nice to someone: The visitors all complimented the choice of furnishings.

**CONSCIENCE/CONSCIENTIOUS/CONSCIOUS

Your **conscience** is your sense of right and wrong (literally "the thing you know with").

If you are **conscientious**, you do things diligently and with a serious sense of duty.

If you are **conscious**, you are aware.

*CONSTRAINTS/RESTRAINTS

constraints fence you in.

restraints hold you back.

*CONTRADICT/CONTRAVENE

You **contradict** someone when you tell them they're wrong.

You **contravene** a law or regulation when you disobey it.

***COUNCIL/COUNSEL

A **council** is a group of advisors or decision-makers. It is the spelling to use in "council of war".

counsel is advice, or (in the phrase "legal counsel"), someone who gives advice.

***CORONATION/CROWNED

A **coronation** is the ceremony in which a monarch is **crowned**. They are not ~~coronated~~; there is no such word.

**COURTESAN/COURTIER

Although **courtesan** did start life meaning the same as **courtier** (a member of the nobility who attends the king's court), it no longer means that; "courtesan" refers to a woman who makes her living by being a professional mistress to wealthy men.

**CREVASSE/CREVICE

A **crevasse** is a large vertical gap in the landscape, often in ice.

A **crevice** is a small or narrow gap or crack.

*CUBICAL/CUBICLE

cubical is an adjective, meaning shaped like a cube.

A **cubicle** is what Dilbert works in.

***CUE/QUEUE

A **cue** is a signal, often to an actor: "I have to go on, that's my cue." You also cue up a song on a playlist.

A **queue** is a line where you wait for something: "He stood in the queue for hours."

*CREAK/CREEK

A **creak** is the kind of noise a door makes if its hinges aren't well oiled.

A **creek** is a stream, usually muddy.

*DAMMED/DAMNED

If something is **dammed**, it's prevented from flowing (like a river).

If it's **damned**, it's destined for an eternity in hell (or, metaphorically, is annoying).

*DEFINITELY/DEFINITIVELY

definitely means "for sure": He definitely used the wrong word there.

definitively means "in a way that involves formal definition": The province passed definitively into the control of the Teutonic Knights after the Battle of Kamerlin. Increasingly, people write "definitively" when they mean "definitely".

****DEFUSE/DIFFUSE

defuse refers to preventing a bomb from going off.

diffuse means to spread small particles over a wide area, which is one possible consequence of not defusing a bomb.

You defuse a situation, you do not ~~diffuse~~ it.

**DENY/DISPUTE/REFUTE

If you **deny** an accusation, you are claiming it isn't true.

If you **dispute** an accusation, you are arguing that it isn't true.

If you **refute** an accusation, you are proving it isn't true.

Some people use *refute* when they mean *deny* or *dispute*.

**DESERT/DESSERT

The spelling **desert** is pronounced two different ways.

With the emphasis on the first syllable, it means a dry, arid area (the Sahara Desert).

With the emphasis on the second syllable, it's a verb meaning to leave in a way that causes problems for those left behind.

It's also used as a noun in the phrase "just deserts," meaning what someone justly deserves.

Rhyming with the second pronunciation, but spelled differently, **dessert** is the sweet course of a meal.

*DETRACT/DISTRACT

If something **detracts** from something else, it makes it less appealing.

If it **distracts**, it takes attention away from it.

*DINGHY/DINGY

A **dinghy** is a small rowing boat (or rowboat, if you're American). The usual pronunciation rhymes with "thingy".

dingy rhymes with "cringy" and is an adjective that means dull and badly lit.

*DISBURSE/DISPERSE

You **disburse** a sum of money. The "burse" part of the word is related to "purse" (both come from the Latin for a money bag), hence "bursar" (a university official who handles finances) and "bursary" (a form of financial assistance for study).

The similarly-pronounced word **disperse** means to take a group of similar things and cause them to spread out to the point that the group no longer exists: The police dispersed the crowd.

****DISCREET/DISCRETE

discreet means "not drawing unnecessary attention": I trust you to be discreet about the unicorns in the basement.

discrete means "separate": The information was transmitted in discrete packets.

There's a simple test for this pair. "Indiscreet" is the opposite of "discreet", and will be in your spellcheck dictionary, but there's no such word as "~~indiscrete~~". Put an "in" on the front, and if spellcheck queries it, you have the one that means "separate".

Another way to remember: the T in "discrete" keeps the two Es discrete.

*DIVOT/RIVET

A **divot** is a small chunk taken out of something, often a piece of grassy ground, like on a golf course.

A **rivet** is a small metal pin that holds two pieces of metal together.

**ADORN/DON/WEAR

To **adorn** something means to decorate it, not to put it on. You can adorn yourself with it by putting it on, though.

To **don** something means to put it on. It's short for "do on," and there's a less-commonly-used opposite, *doff*, short for "do off". It's old-fashioned.

To don does not mean "to wear".

*DOSE/DOZE

A **dose** is a measure of medicine.

A **doze** is a light sleep.

**DOUSE/DOWSE

You **dowse** with a divining rod in order to locate water.

Once you find the water, you can **douse** things with it (make them wet).

The second meaning sometimes got the "w" spelling in the 19th and early 20th centuries, but that spelling is now considered incorrect.

**DRAW/DRAWER

To **draw** is to create a picture, or to pull or attract.

The sliding thing in a piece of furniture that you keep things in is spelled **drawer**, even though the two words are pronounced the same (in some dialects of English, at least).

*EKE/EEK

The word **eke** is now used only in the expression "to eke out," meaning to make something last by careful and ungenerous use of it.

eek is an exclamation that a person seeing a mouse might stereotypically make.

**ELICIT/ILLICIT

If you **elicit** something you draw it out. Compare *escape* and *emerge*. It is a verb.

If something is **illicit** you are not supposed to have it. Compare *illegal*. It is an adjective.

***EMINENT/IMMANENT/IMMINENT

eminent means "prominent and respected in one's field".

immanent means "inherent".

imminent means "about to happen".

**ENDEAR

You **endear yourself to** someone, you don't ~~endear them~~.

**ENVELOP/ENVELOPE

envelop is the verb: I expect her to envelop me in a hug.

envelope is the noun: I put it in an envelope.

***ERSTWHILE

erstwhile means "former": her erstwhile lover was now banned from the premises.

I often see it used to mean... I'm not sure what, but definitely not "former". Perhaps "would-be" or "supposed"?

****EVERY DAY/EVERYDAY

every day is an adverbial phrase, and refers to repetition on a daily basis: He bought a coffee every day. (That's how he bought it: he bought it every day.) If you could substitute "each day," or if it's parallel to "every week," you need the space between the two words.

everyday is an adjective: Drinking coffee was an everyday event. (That's what kind of event it was: it was an everyday event.)

I discuss this and other similar pairs in more detail in the section on Open and closed pairs, below.

*EXORBITANT/EXTRAVAGANT

An excessively high price is **exorbitant** (but a very large number that is unrelated to charging you money is not).

People who waste their money, especially on luxuries, are **extravagant**.

*FAIN/FEIGN

fain is an old-fashioned word, mostly used in expressions like "I would fain depart," meaning "I would like to leave".

If you **feign** something, you're pretending or faking.

*FAINT/FEINT

If you **faint**, you have passed out. This is also the spelling where something isn't strong ("a faint accent").

If you **feint**, you have made a movement to fool someone into thinking you are going to attack.

***FAIR/FARE

Both of these words have multiple meanings.

The spelling **fair** can mean: treating people equitably; pale ("fair hair"); good-looking (an old-fashioned meaning now); good, as in "fair weather"; reasonable, as in "a fair amount"; just OK, as in "a fair performance"; a temporary event with booths, stalls, etc. (Renaissance fair, county fair).

The spelling **fare** can mean: something you eat ("good fare", somewhat old-fashioned); a charge to travel, as in "taxi fare", or the person who pays that charge, as in "he picked up a fare uptown"; to travel, go, or get along (as in the expression "farewell", also somewhat old-fashioned), which is the source of the "charge for travel" meaning.

****FAZE/PHASE

If something doesn't **faze** you it leaves you cool, calm and collected.

If it doesn't **phase** you, you are probably in a superhero novel, and have just avoided being made immaterial and pushed through a wall.

****FLAIR/FLARE

If you have a **flair**, you have a notable talent.

If you have a **flare**, you have a kind of firework used for signalling, or something that starts out narrow and gets wider.

*FLAUNT/FLOUT

You **flaunt** something when you show it off in an ostentatious manner.

You **flout** a rule or authority or convention when you defy it.

**FLOW/FLOE

flow refers to water (or something similar) moving from place to place: *a lava flow*.

floe specifically means an ice floe, a sheet of floating ice.

****FLUSH OUT/FLESH OUT**

You **flush out** an animal from the bushes (drive it out of hiding).

You **flesh out** a proposal (take it from a basic or bare-bones state to being more developed).

****FORWARD/FOREWORD**

forward is the opposite of **backward**.

A **foreword** is an author's note at the beginning of a book. Look at the elements it's made up of: *fore*, as in before, and *word*.

Likewise **afterward** and **afterword**.

***GAMBIT/GAMUT/GAUNTLET**

A **gambit** is an initial move in chess or some other strategic context.

If you **run the gamut**, you are covering the range between either two specified points or, if no points are specified, across the entire possible range:

"This author's writing runs the gamut from mediocre all the way to competent."

"I ran the gamut of emotions."

If you **run the gauntlet**, you are either passing between two rows of people who are hitting you, typically with sticks, as a military punishment or trial of courage; or, metaphorically, you are undergoing a public humiliation or a series of difficult trials.

There is no phrase ~~run the gambit~~. It is a confusion with one of the other two words, usually *gamut*.

**GLANCE AT/GLIMPSE

You **glimpse** something (see it for a moment); you **glance at** something (look at it briefly or indirectly).

I've also seen sentences like "~~She glimpsed over her shoulder~~"; that should be "glanced," because "glimpsed" needs an object: "She glimpsed *him* over her shoulder." And the reverse: "~~She glanced the woman~~," when it should be either "She glanced at the woman" or "She glimpsed the woman."

*GRILL/GRILLE

grill is a verb: *I grilled the burger*, or a noun: *I cooked it on the grill*. It relates to cooking, though there is also the metaphorical sense of "interrogate".

grille is always a noun, and refers typically to crosshatched metal with gaps in it, like a grating.

***GRISLY/GRISTLY/GRIZZLY

A **grisly** death is a horrible and distressing one.

A **gristly** death involves a lot of gristle.

A **grizzly** death involves a bear (or complaining in a whiny manner).

**GUARDIAN/WARD

An adult who is legally responsible for a child who is not their biological child is a **guardian**. The child is their **ward**.

The adult in this situation is not the ward.

*HAWK/HOCK

If you're **hawking** an item, you are offering it for sale, probably in an open-air market or in the street.

If you're **hocking** it, you are placing it with a pawnbroker.

Either one can be used if you're gathering saliva in preparation for spitting.

*HEAL/HEEL

heal means to restore someone's health: It took his wound a long time to heal.

heel is the back part of your foot: He was wounded in the heel.

***HEAR, HEAR

If you say "**hear, hear!**" in response to someone's speech, you are expressing enthusiastic approval by encouraging those around you to listen to what he or she is saying. The full expression was originally "hear him!".

Do not spell it "~~here~~" in this context.

*HEARTY/HARDY

Probably the result of American pronunciation ambiguity ("t" and "d" in the middle of words are pronounced almost the same in some US dialects).

Someone who is **hearty** is cheerful and outgoing.

Someone who is **hardy** is resilient and tough.

***HENCE/HITHER/THENCE/THITHER/WHENCE/WHITHER/WITHER

hence means "from here".

hither means "to here".

thence means "from there".

thither means "to there".

whence means "from where".

whither means "to where".

wither (with no "h") means to dry up like a dead leaf.

I have seen even good writers, who should know better, get these confused.

*HEW/HUE

To **hew** something is to cut it, often with an axe. It's an old-fashioned word.

A **hue** is a color or shade. That's also the spelling used in the old expression "hue and cry," meaning a public outcry or loud commotion; originally, this had a legal meaning relating to the pursuit of criminals.

***HOARD/HORDE

A **hoard** is a collection of precious objects.

A **horde** is a group of dangerous beings.

**HOME IN ON/HONE IN ON

Both of this pair are in common usage, and some consider both to be correct. "Home in on" is about 10 years older, according to Merriam-Webster, dating from the 1950s, and is the much more common usage and (therefore) the one that is less likely to be considered incorrect. Both are metaphors: **home in on** is based on the "homing" ability of a missile, derived in turn from that of a pigeon, while **hone in on** is a metaphor about sharpening one's focus, a hone being a sharpening stone. The distinction is subtle, similar to *leach* versus *leech*.

*HONORARIUM/HONORIFIC

An **honorarium** is a small sum of money paid to an otherwise unpaid officeholder, to compensate them for expenses incurred in holding the office.

An **honorific** is similar to a title, and is added to someone's name to indicate that they hold a particular honour.

***HURDLE/HURL/HURTLE

You **hurdle** something if you jump over it.

You **hurl** it if you throw it.

You **hurtle** if you're moving rapidly.

****IMPLY/INFER

If you **imply** something, your words subtly indicate it: He implied that she was drunk at the time by mentioning her liking for tequila.

If you **infer** something, you come to a conclusion based on indirect evidence: He inferred that she was drunk based on her slurred speech.

Both of them contain the idea of indirectness, but *imply* is creating an impression in the minds of others, *infer* is coming to a conclusion in your own mind.

**INCIDENCE/INCIDENT/INSTANCE/INSTANT

incidence is how frequently an undesirable thing happens: The incidence of violent crime in the city is decreasing.

An **incident** is usually a one-off event, with an implication that it's not desired or unfortunate or at least dramatic: The Noodle Incident.

An **instance** is one of a number of similar things: This is an instance of exactly what I'm talking about!

An **instant** is a moment in time: I blacked out for an instant.

**INCREDIBLE/INCREDULOUS

An amazing thing is **incredible**.

If I don't believe you, I am **incredulous**. (Unlike "incredible," which seldom means "unbelievable" now in a literal sense, "incredulous" keeps its original meaning of "not believing".)

**INTER/INTERN

If you **inter** people, you bury them in graves.

If you **intern** them, you lock them up to prevent them possibly causing harm.

***INTO/IN TO

If you turn criminals **in to** the authorities, you're helping to keep society safe.

If you turn criminals **into** the authorities, you'll have a very different kind of society.

"Into" and "onto" are correct if you are talking about movement, but don't use them if you're writing a phrase that ends in "in" or "on" and happens to be followed by "to". See Prepositions.

****JAM/JAMB**

A **jam** is a kind of preserve made with sugar and, usually, fruit.

A **jamb** is the vertical piece at the side of a door.

*****JOURNEY/SOJOURN**

A **journey** means moving from one place to another.

A **sojourn** means staying in one place for a while. It is not a fancy word for "journey". It means the exact opposite.

***KNELL/KNOLL**

A **knell** is the sound of a bell being tolled for a funeral.

A **knoll** is a small rise in the ground.

*****LEACH/LEECH**

It's often difficult to know exactly when to use each of these two, since they work in similar contexts, especially when used metaphorically.

leach usually means that something is being washed out by water: The calcium was being leached from the rock.

leech means that something is being sucked out (by analogy to a leech, a blood-sucking creature): The party leeched the energy out of me.

******LED/LEAD**

This is a confusing pair because of both meaning and pronunciation.

led (pronounced to rhyme with Ted) is the past tense form of lead (pronounced to rhyme with seed).

lead (pronounced to rhyme with Ted) is the soft grey metal that alchemists tried to turn into gold.

**LEANT/LENT

leant is the past tense of lean (an alternative form of leaned).

lent is the past tense of lend (an alternative form of loaned, if you like), and also the period before Easter.

*LEFT OVER/LEFTOVER

If something is **left over** (adjective), it remains at the end of, for example, a meal.

A **leftover** (noun), more often **leftovers**, refers to the food that remains after a meal is eaten. See below for more Open and Closed Pairs.

**LEST/UNLESS

These two words are not synonyms. "Lest" has a specific meaning of its own, and is most familiar in the phrase "lest we forget"; it means that you are taking some action in order to prevent a bad outcome.

**LEVER/LEVERAGE

lever is usually literal: He levered the rock off his friend.

leverage (as a verb) is usually figurative: He leveraged his advantage into a win.

****LOATH/LOATHE

loath means reluctant or unwilling: I am loath to do anything that would strengthen her position.

loathe means to dislike strongly, despise: I loathe her and her whole family.

*MANOR/MANNER

A **manor** is a large country house, or, in British police slang, a geographical area of responsibility: I don't take to this kind of thing on my manor, see?

A **manner** is the kind of outward attitude taken towards something: I don't like your manner.

Shakespeare's phrase "to the manner born" (Hamlet, Act I, Scene 4) means accustomed through being brought up to a certain way of doing things; it's sometimes, as a pun, rendered "to the manor born," implying being brought up to wealth and privilege.

**MARSHAL/MARTIAL/MARSHALL

martial is an adjective, meaning "warlike".

A **marshal** is an officer.

Marshall is a surname (based on the title of marshal). Don't spell the title with a second "l". It's like Taylor and Abbott; the surname retains an older spelling that has been abandoned for the noun.

**MAY BE/MAYBE

The phrase **may be** indicates that something is possible: "That may be the biggest dog I ever saw." You could substitute "could be", "might be" or "has to be" and the sentence would still make sense.

The single word **maybe** indicates neither "yes" nor "no": "Maybe I've seen a bigger one; maybe I haven't." You could substitute "perhaps" and the sentence would still make sense.

*MAYHAP/PERHAPS

If you absolutely insist on using old-fashioned language, despite the fact that it's almost always a bad idea, **mayhap** is a synonym for **perhaps**. Do not spell it ~~mayhaps~~ (importing the "s" from "perhaps").

*METAL/METTLE

If you show someone your **metal**, you are showing them iron, gold, silver, etc.

If you show them your **mettle**, you are demonstrating your ability.

**MIGHT/MITE

If you mean a small amount, that's a **mite**, not a ~~might~~. **Might** means strength.

**MORAL/MORALE

moral means concerned with doing the right thing.

morale is the spirit of a group of people, usually military.

****MUCOUS/MUCUS

mucous is the adjective: His mucous membranes were dried out.

mucus is the noun: Mucus dripped from his mouth.

**NONPLUSSED

nonplussed means surprised, stunned.

Unfortunately, some people have started using it to mean the exact opposite (unfazed), and this usage is becoming common enough that the word is probably going to lose its usefulness, because you won't know which of the two opposite meanings is intended.

**OMNIPOTENT/OMNISCIENT

If you are **omnipotent**, you are all-powerful. Compare "potent".

If you are **omniscient**, you know everything. Compare "science".

If your narrator is able to look into the heads of all the characters and know things they don't know, that is an *omniscient* narrator. There is no such thing as an ~~omnipotent narrator~~.

**OPAQUE/TRANSLUCENT/TRANSPARENT

If something is **opaque**, you cannot see through it at all, like something made of solid steel.

If it is **translucent**, you can see light shining through it but can't see what's on the other side, like clouded glass used for a bathroom window.

If it is **transparent**, you can see right through it, like clear glass. Some people write "opaque" when they mean "transparent" (the opposite of opaque).

**PALATE/PALLET/PALETTE

Your **palate** is in your mouth, or metaphorically refers to your ability to taste.

A **pallet** is a flat object used to make transporting goods easier, or a makeshift bed made up on the floor.

A **palette** is a flat piece of wood used by an artist to mix colours, or, by extension, a selection of colours (*the room was decorated in a muted palette of greys*).

****PALPATE/PALPITATE**

If you **palpate** something, you squeeze it.

A heart **palpitates**, meaning it beats so hard you can feel it.

****PASSED/PAST**

passed means gone by: Many years had passed.

past is the time before the present: In the past, we haven't allowed that.

Note also the expression "pastime", meaning a way of passing the time. It should not be written as "~~passed time~~".

*****PEAK/PEEK/PIQUE**

A **peak** is the top of something, usually a mountain: Sir Edmund struggled to the peak of Everest.

A **peek** is a quick look: He took a peek out of the tent. (This is the one to use for "sneak peek," which people often get wrong—probably because the correct spelling involves spelling the same sound two different ways in consecutive words.)

There are also the phrases "to **pique** one's interest" and "a fit of **pique**", both of which are spelled with a Q.

*****PEAL/PEEL**

A **peal** is a loud sound, usually made by a bell or thunder.

A **peel** is a rind around a fruit.

The expression "peel off" uses the "fruit" spelling. It's a dead metaphor.

**PEDAL/PEDDLE

If you **pedal** something, it is probably a bicycle or something very like one.

If you **peddle** it, you are selling it on the street. (It could still be a bicycle, I suppose.)

**PENDANT/PENDENT

A **pendant** is a piece of jewellery you hang around your neck on a chain.

pendent is an adjective, meaning "hanging".

**PERPETRATE/PERPETUATE

You **perpetrate** a crime.

You **perpetuate** an injustice (make it perpetual).

**PERQUISITE/PREREQUISITE

A **perquisite** is a benefit, often obtained through one's position.

A **prerequisite** is something that you need in order to get something else.

**PHOSPHOROUS/PHOSPHORUS

As in many other cases (compare mucous/mucus), the -ous version is an adjective and the -us version is a noun.

**PLAIN/PLANE

A **plain** is a large natural area of flat ground.

A **plane** is an abstract flat area (among other definitions).

****POO-POO/POOH-POOH**

If you dismiss something contemptuously, you **pooh-pooh** it.

poo-pooing it is more drastic, and implies you have swallowed it first.

****POPULACE/POPULOUS**

populace is a noun. It means the people who populate a place.

populous is an adjective. It means that a lot of people live there.

******PORE/POUR**

You don't **pour** over a book or paper (unless you are dousing it in liquid, in which case you need to specify what you're pouring over it). You **pore** over it.

***PRECEDE/PROCEED**

To **precede** someone means to go in front of them.

To **proceed** means to carry on.

*****PRECEDENCE/PRECEDENT**

precedence refers to the rules about who is considered more important than whom socially: a duke takes precedence over an earl. It's also used for other hierarchies of importance and priority: safety takes precedence over speed.

precedent is usually a legal term, meaning that a similar case has been decided in the past.

**PREDOMINANT/PROMINENT/DOMINANT

Something is **predominant** if it is the most common type of whatever it is: The predominant religion in the Southern USA is Protestantism.

Something or someone is **prominent** if it is well-known or influential.

Something or someone is **dominant** if it dominates others.

****PREMIER/PREMIERE

premier (with no e on the end) means first in the sense of pre-eminent; with a capital, it's also a title equivalent to Prime Minister.

A **premiere** (with an e on the end) is the first showing of a movie, performance of a play, etc.

****PRESCRIBE/PROSCRIBE

If you **prescribe** something you require it.

If you **proscribe** something you forbid it.

The words are opposites.

****PRINCIPAL/PRINCIPLE

principal means primary: The principal exports of Peru. It also means a person in charge of a school.

principle is an abstract idea used to guide actions: The principle of the greatest good for the greatest number.

*PRODIGY/PROTEGE

A **prodigy** is a (typically young) person who is unusually good at something.

A **protege** is someone who is mentored or sponsored by another person, usually older, who possesses some influence.

**PRODUCE/PRODUCT

This one depends in part on what dictionary you look at. Everyone will agree that fruits and vegetables are **produce** (the noun, pronounced with the stress on the first syllable, to distinguish it from the verb with the same spelling, which takes the stress on the second syllable). "Fruit and vegetables" is the normal and most common meaning. Some will say that produce is anything produced on a farm, including dairy, meat, or grain, but that it's always something edible. Most would agree that something someone has made that is not food from a farm is a **product**, not produce, but Merriam-Webster suggests that anything someone produces is their produce, and even puts that definition before the "comes from a farm" one. I recommend keeping "produce" for fruit and vegetables and calling anything else a "product". I'm thinking in particular of an ice cream seller in one book I read who referred to his ice cream as his "produce," though he was selling it, not making it; to me, that's clearly his "product".

***PROPHECY/PROPHESY

A **prophecy** is a prediction of the future (in common usage, anyway; a Bible scholar will have a slightly different definition): I return, in accordance with the prophecy!

To **prophesy** is to speak a prophecy.

There is no such word as "~~prophesize~~".

**PUS/PUSS

pus is the unpleasant matter that forms in an infected wound.

puss is something you call a cat.

This seems like a rare exception to the usual rule for short and long vowels and single and double consonants, though these are nouns, and that rule applies to verbs or adjectives formed from verbs. See Double Letters and Pronunciation.

*RECANT/RECOUNT

You **recant** your testimony if you claim that you were mistaken or lying.

You **recount** a story (meaning you tell it).

**REIGNS/REINS/RAINS

reigns are associated with kings and queens.

reins are associated with horses.

rains are associated with the band Toto and their song "Africa," and refer to water falling from the sky.

**RELISH/REVEL IN/REJOICE IN

You can **relish** something delightful, or **revel in** it, or **rejoice in** it, but you do not ~~relish in~~ it.

***RETCH/WRETCH

To **retch** is to gag or vomit: He retched up his dinner.

A **wretch** is an unfortunate or despicable person: The poor wretch is starving.

*RIFLING/RIFFLING/RIFFING

If someone is **rifling** through some papers, they are probably searching for something to steal.

If they are **riffling** through the papers, they are turning them over quickly and casually.

If they are **riffing**, they are improvising on a jazz tune.

***RIGHT/RITE

A **right** is a moral or legal entitlement, as in "right to free speech".

A **rite** is a ceremony, as in "rite of passage".

**RIGOROUS/VIGOROUS

If you do something **rigorously**, you do it thoroughly and with attention to detail. If you do it **vigorously**, you do it with a lot of energy.

*RING/WRING

A telephone **rings**. It has a **ringer**. A near-twin is a **dead ringer**.

You **wring** out washing by squeezing it (possibly with a **wringer**, as in the expression "put through the wringer"). You also **wring your hands**.

**ROLE/ROLL

A **role** is a part that you play, such as in a movie.

A list of the students who should be in a classroom is a **roll**, and so is a movement where something tumbles over and over.

*SCRAP/SCRAPE

A **scrap** is a small piece of something, or, colloquially, a fight.

A **scrape** is an injury or damage caused by friction, or, colloquially, a situation involving danger and conflict (but not usually actual fighting).

**SECRET/SECRETE

secret means hidden or not generally known: She hid in the secret passage.

secrete means to hide: He secreted the treasure under the floorboards.

Secrete also means to produce, usually some kind of fluid: The frogs secrete poison from their skins.

*SEAM/SEEM

A **seam** is where two pieces of cloth are stitched together (or other materials are joined in a similar way).

To **seem** means to appear; there is no noun spelled that way.

**SENSIBILITY

Sensibility is not the quality of being level-headed. It means being sensitive or alert to nuances.

**SEW/SOW

To **sew** means to join together with a needle and thread.

To **sow** means to plant seeds.

***SHEAR/SHEER

sheer means you can see through it, usually applied to women's clothing: She wore a sheer silk nightgown. It also means "very steep": The sheer cliff loomed above them. And it's occasionally used as an intensifier: The sheer effrontery of his suggestion enraged her.

As a verb, "sheer" is used like this: He sheered away from the cliff; He sheered off down a little-used road.

shears are scissors: He cut the silk with his shears.

As a verb, "shear" is used in the sense of cutting: He sheared away (or sheared off) some of the excess.

There's "wind shear" as well, and other "shear forces", meaning forces that push at an angle.

Your best move if you want to use one or other of these words is to check the dictionary to make sure you've picked the right one.

**SHEATH/SHEATHE

This pair works like breath/breathe.

sheath is the noun: He put the sword in its sheath.

sheathe is the verb: He decided to sheathe the sword.

*SHONE/SHOWN

In some US dialects, these words are pronounced the same, and speakers of those dialects occasionally confuse them.

shone is the past tense of shine. "Shined" is an alternative, which means the same.

shown is the past tense of show, but only in the perfect tense or passive voice.

He *showed* me the door (simple past tense).

He *has shown* me the door (present perfect tense).

He *had shown* me the door (past perfect tense).

I *was shown* the door (passive voice).

It's not standard English to say "~~He shown me the door~~" or "~~I was showed the door~~"; you could probably get away with "he has/had showed me the door," but *shown* is preferable.

***SIGHT/SITE

sight is the sense you use to see with, or something you see with it. It is also used for a rifle sight (which you see through).

A **site** is a place (including a web site).

**SILICON/SILICONE

silicon is an element, a component of sand and rock (and silicon chips).

silicone is a type of plastic, used for cookware and breast implants, among other things.

*SINGULAR/SINGLE

If you mean **single** (in a group of one), don't write **singular** (distinctively unlike others, or specifically characterized by not being plural).

*SLATHER/SLAVER

To **slather** means to generously apply a substance, usually greasy, to a surface: He slathered his face with sunscreen.

To **slaver** means to drool in a ravenous manner: Pavlov's dogs slavered at the sound of the bell.

*SLOG/SLUDGE/TRUDGE

To **slog** is to progress with tedious difficulty.

To **trudge** is to walk in a weary manner.

I have seen people (presumably) merge these words into **sludge**, which means something quite different: it's a noun referring to an unpleasant substance with the consistency of thick mud. It's not a verb.

*SLEIGHT/SLIGHT

The word **sleight** is almost solely used in the phrase "sleight of hand".

slight means small or slender; it can also refer to an insult (which dismisses someone as small or unimportant).

*SLOPING/SLOPPING

See the discussion below of Double Letters and Pronunciation.

*SNUGGLY/SNUGLY

snuggly is an adjective that suggests something or someone (probably a child or an animal) is enjoying snuggling up. They are being snuggly.

snugly refers to how something fits; if it fits snugly, the fit is tight.

*SOLE/SOUL

A **sole** is the bottom part of a shoe (or a kind of flatfish). It also means "alone".

A **soul** is the part of yourself that isn't your body.

**SOME TIME/SOMETIME

some time means "an amount of time": Some time had passed since he'd been there.

sometime means "at an indefinite time": He'd go there sometime, he was sure of it.

Compare: any more/anymore, every day/everyday. These pairs are discussed further in Open and Closed Pairs.

*STAID/STAYED

staid means steady, with an implication of old-fashioned and fuddy-duddy: The staid old man refused to get a cellphone.

stayed is the past tense of stay: He stayed in the same house for fifty years.

*STEAL/STEEL

You **steal** an object, if you are a thief.

You **steel** your resolve if you expect to face difficulties.

*STRAIGHT/STRAIT

straight means aligned, as in "a straight line".

A **strait** is a narrow point in the sea.

The expression "in dire straits" uses the narrow-point meaning metaphorically to mean "in a challenging situation".

**STRIPPED/STRIPED

If someone is **stripped** they have had their clothes removed.

If something is **striped** it has alternating bands of color.

See the discussion below on Double Letters and Pronunciation.

****SUBSTANTIAL/SUBSTANTIVE**

substantial means that the thing has substance, and implies that it's large, solid, ample, strong, etc. A substantial thing is tangible or real.

substantive means actual or essential, or having importance and effect, but is more abstract than "substantial" and does not carry as clear an implication of solidity, tangibility, largeness or strength.

Use "substantial" if you're referring to a physical thing. Arguments can be substantive; houses can be substantial.

***TACK/TACT**

A **tack** can be a small nail, a direction taken when sailing against the wind, or (metaphorically, based on the previous meaning) a way of proceeding: So that's the tack you intend to take, is it?

tact is the quality a diplomat should be notable for.

*****TAUNT/TAUT/TAUGHT**

taunt is something you do when you mock someone.

taut means tight: The taut muscles of his stomach rippled.

taught is the past tense of teach.

*****TENANTS/TENETS**

tenants rent a building.

tenets are beliefs that you hold.

***TIC/TICK

A **tic** is a twitch, usually repetitive, or, metaphorically, an unconscious habit.

A **tick** is a bloodsucking creature, the sound a clock makes, or, in British English, what Americans call a checkmark.

**TIMBER/TIMBRE

timber is wood.

timbre is the quality that makes one musical instrument (or voice) distinct from another.

***TOUSLE/TUSSLE

tousle means to mess up, usually someone's hair.

tussle means to wrestle.

***TROOP/TROUPE

Soldiers form a **troop**.

Performers form a **troupe**.

A troop can shoot at you, but a troupe can only shout at you.

**TUFF/TUFT

tuff is rock composed of volcanic ash that has been compressed.

A **tuft** is a small clump of hair, feathers, cloth etc. that stands out from its surroundings.

*TUILE/TULLE/TWILL

A **tuile** is a very thin, crispy wafer you might get in a high-end dessert.

A **tulle** is a thin, diaphanous net fabric. It's like a tuile in that both are lacy; it's unlike it in that a tulle is not generally edible and a tuile is not generally wearable.

A **twill** is a cloth woven in such a way that diagonal lines run through it.

**ULULATING/UNDULATING

A cry can be described as **ululating**, meaning it goes up and down in pitch (think of the classic Tarzan yell as practiced by Johnny Weissmuller).

A landscape can be described as **undulating**, meaning that it goes up and down in height.

*UPMOST/UTMOST

Something that is **upmost** is at the top, uppermost. You do your **utmost** (not your ~~upmost~~) to succeed.

**VOUCHSAFE

The word **vouchsafe** sounds like it means to assure or guarantee something, but it does not; it means to confide secret information or hand over something valuable to be taken care of.

***WAIL/WALE/WHALE

wail means to make a loud, high-pitched noise.

wale (as a verb) means to make long thin marks.

whale (as a verb) means to hit hard and repeatedly. This is the one you want when someone is "whaling on" someone else.

***WAIVER/WAVER

A **waiver** is something you sign to give up your right to sue.

If you **waver**, you are going back and forth, like a wave.

*WANGLE/WRANGLE

To **wangle** is to use any influence or persuasiveness you possess to obtain something.

To **wrangle** is to round up cattle, or do something metaphorically similar to rounding up cattle (like directing employees).

*WICKER/WHICKER

wicker is what baskets are woven from.

A **whicker** is a noise a horse makes.

*WRAP/RAP

You **wrap** a present in paper.

You **rap** on a door.

Opposite Meanings Sometimes Confused

English words sometimes change their sense over the years from positive to negative or vice versa. *Condescension*, for example, was once positive, as was *awful*. And there are words like *literally*, which now also means *figuratively* ("my head literally exploded"), or rather is used for emphasis or intensity rather than for its... literal meaning. I don't propose to go into these examples in depth; some people who think of themselves as language purists will get sniffy about some of them (like *literally*), and I do agree that in some cases there's a loss of meaning or distinction when a word like *enormity* (meaning a truly terrible act) becomes confused with *enormousness*, meaning we now have no single word for what *enormity* used to mean. Not that we used it often, which is why it was able to drift to the meaning of *enormousness*, and I'm honestly happier with a world where we don't need to use it too often.

Disinterested is also often used to mean *uninterested*, though the original meaning was *unbiased*. There, at least, we have *unbiased* to fall back on.

Words like this are sometimes called "skunked terms," a name that originated in *Garner's Modern English Usage*, meaning that they may need to be avoided because people are no longer sure which of the meanings is intended.

Language moves on, and there's nothing we can do about it; people have been getting uptight about changes in language for centuries, with minimal impact on actual usage in most cases. I'm more concerned here with words like the examples I've given in the main list above, where people occasionally slip up with what is still the majority usage.

There is also a phenomenon in English where the same word can mean two opposite things. There's even a word for it: these are "contronyms". Sometimes these are two words that were originally separate and have converged on the same spelling, like *cleave*, which can mean either separate or join together. Sometimes they are the result of turning a noun into a verb, such as *dust*, which can mean remove dust (from a house) or add something resembling dust (such as icing sugar on a cake).

Sometimes, though, people just remember vaguely that a word is in the general realm of what they mean, but not that it means the opposite of what they mean. I have several examples of this in the list above:

- Ancestor vs descendant

- Guardian vs ward

- Opaque vs transparent

There are also *prescribe* and *proscribe*, which are opposites that are spelled very similarly, as are *belie* and *betray*.

Imply and *infer* are not strictly opposites in meaning, but they definitely mean different things and are easily confused for each other.

Journey and *sojourn*, because they share a syllable, are often thought to mean the same thing, but they do not; a sojourn is a period of staying in one place, the opposite of a journey. It's an old-fashioned word, and may be in danger of getting skunked, though context usually tells you whether someone was travelling or staying put.

And then there's *nonplussed*, which means so startled as to be unable to react for a moment, but which some people have started to use as if it means *unfazed*, the exact opposite. I have even seen a writer who normally makes very few mistakes make this one. It may be getting skunked; we shall see.

Double Letters and Pronunciation

I include an entry above for sloping/slopping, having read a book recently where the author repeatedly referred to "a slopping roof" when she meant "sloping". I've seen other similar errors occasionally, where an author will use a double consonant where it should be single or vice versa, such as *robbed* where the author meant *robed*, or *scrapping* confused with *scraping*, *stripping* with *striping* or *dolled* with *doled*.

There's a (mostly) consistent rule, for once. Slope/sloping/sloped has a long vowel, ends in an "e" in its base form and takes a single consonant in the "-ing" or "-ed" form; slop/slopping/slopped has a short vowel, no terminal "e" in its base form and a double consonant. Compare *rope* (roping, roped), which ends in e, and *shop* (shopping, shopped) which does not.

> *If the base form ends in -e, the vowel is long, and the consonant is single in the -ed and -ing forms.*

> *If the base form does not end in -e, the vowel is short, and the consonant is double in the -ed and -ing forms.*

There's a similar issue with double vowels sometimes, such as *loose* (long vowel) versus *lose* (short vowel). Here, it's a bit easier to tell which are supposed to be long and which are supposed to be short: the long ones are doubled.

Confusable Adverbs

Based on the fact that I see people confusing them, there are certain adjective forms that are easily confused. They seem to involve the ending *-fully*.

If you do something *purposefully* you do it in a way that's full of purpose, determined. This is different from doing it *purposely*, that is, intentionally.

Likewise, if you *wrongly* accuse someone, you were incorrect in your accusation, but if you *wrongfully* accuse them, you had no right to do so.

Into and in to

I mention this above under Commonly Confused Words, but it's worth discussing in slightly more depth. There's a difference between "turning criminals in to the authorities" and "turning criminals into the authorities". The first means that you are handing the criminals over to the authorities, while the second means that the criminals are becoming the authorities.

Consider parallel phrases: "turn them in / for punishment" or "hand them over / to the authorities". Just because two prepositions (such as "in" and "to") happen to be neighbours in a phrase is no reason for them to merge together and become a different preposition ("into").

The same issue sometimes occurs with "onto". "He jumped onto the box," but "My friend put me on to a good deal," which is equivalent to "My friend introduced me to a good deal". The "to" belongs to the phrase "to a good deal" and should not be merged in a single word with the "on".

Open and closed pairs

There are several examples in English of pairs that mean one thing when they are styled open (with a space between them) and another thing when they are styled closed (as a single word). For example:

She drank coffee every day.

(Adverbial phrase, modifying "drank".)

A visit to the café was an everyday ritual for her.

(Compound adjective, modifying "ritual".)

However, consider these special cases, which do not follow quite the same pattern. They all involve determiners, which are words that relate to quantity, such as *any*, *some*, or *more*.

Is there any way you can help me?

(Determiner "any" modifying noun "way".)

The cold never bothered me anyway.

(Adverb "anyway" modifying verb "bothered".)

I haven't seen him in some time.

(Determiner "some" modifying noun "time".)

We should look in on him sometime.

(Adverb "sometime" modifying verb phrase "look in".)

I don't want any more beer.

(Determiner "any more" modifying noun "beer"; compare "I want some more beer.")

I don't want beer anymore.

(Adverb "anymore" modifying verb "want".)

"I don't want any more beer" means "I have had enough beer for now". But "I don't want beer anymore" means "I used to want it, but now I don't."

In Britain, both usages of "any more" are frequently styled open, but in the US the adverbial version, referring to something that used to be true but is no longer, is styled closed (*anymore*).

It is incorrect in both dialects to style the non-adverbial version closed:

~~"I don't want anymore beer."~~

Eggcorns and Mangled Idioms

As well as the many examples of outright homonyms I give above, there are also "eggcorns" and other ways of mangling common phrases.

An "eggcorn" (named after the eggcorn for "acorn") is a misspelling based on pronunciation, very like a homonym, but more often for a phrase. Common eggcorns include "~~deep-seeded~~" for "deep-seated," "~~make due~~" for "make do," or "~~for all intensive purposes~~" instead of "for all intents and purposes". They're often a clue that the author doesn't read much, and is writing down a phrase they've only heard spoken, particularly if the mistake is because of a particular dialectal pronunciation. "~~Make due~~," for example, sounds distinctly different from "make do" in many English dialects. Likewise, only an American, speaking a dialect that often voices "t" as "d" in the middle of words, would spell "cuttlefish" as "~~cuddle fish~~".

Other botched expressions I've seen include:

- "~~In of itself~~" or "~~in and itself~~" for "in and of itself"

- "~~All of the sudden~~" for "all of a sudden"

- "~~Vicious circle~~" for "vicious cycle"

- "~~Every each way~~" for "every which way"

- "~~Hung onto dear life~~" for "hung on for dear life"

- "~~If worse comes to worse~~" or "~~If worse comes to worst~~" for "if worst comes to worst" ("if worse comes to worst" is a minority variation that could be defended as correct, since it actually makes sense)

- "~~Worse for the wear~~" for "the worse for wear" (could be a regional variation?)

- "~~Had heard tale~~" for "had heard tell"

- "~~Close-mindedness~~" for "closed-mindedness" (see further discussion under the Adjectives section)

- "~~Hair-brained~~" for "hare-brained" (having the brains of a hare, whose erratic behaviour makes them a metaphor for craziness).

There's a simple way to avoid this kind of error, which is also a good practice in itself: *don't use clichés*. But if you do use an idiom that you haven't seen written down, double-check with a dictionary or online source that you are using the idiom correctly.

Jargon and Pretentious Writing

Speaking of clichés: don't write "going forward" when you mean "in future," "utilise" when you mean "use," or other business jargon of the kind, unless you are representing business people speaking in jargon. Likewise academic or bureaucratic obfuscatory language. Also, don't say "homestead" when you mean "home," "singular" when you mean "single," or "secondary" to mean "second" in an attempt to sound elevated; these words do have different meanings from each other, and rather than sounding elevated you end up sounding ignorant.

It can be difficult, if your day job is in business, bureaucracy, or academia, to get out of the habit of writing that way, but honestly, it's not ideal if you're writing that way in your day job either. Strive to write as clearly and simply as possible and say what you mean; people will appreciate it.

Common Typos

The difference between a typo and the kind of errors I've been talking about up to this point is that the person creating the typo probably knows the rule, knows the correct word to use, but hasn't managed to get their fingers to put down exactly what was in their brain. We all do that from time to time. Some people do it frequently.

Back in the Jurassic Era when I was a copy editor, we still had people called "typesetters" who would take a non-electronic manuscript (typed on a typewriter, or even handwritten) and key it into a computer. They made mistakes, but they made fewer mistakes than some authors do when they type their manuscripts directly into a computer. For better or worse (and probably, on average, for better), those days are gone, and we're all responsible for typing our own manuscripts.

If you're not a very accurate typist, you need to work with that reality and check your work more carefully, though I also suggest that you type more slowly and strive to be accurate in the first place. Maybe take a typing course (there are online ones). Once a mistake is in the manuscript, the chances of even a good editor missing it are about 10%, and if you make hundreds of them that means you'll have tens of errors. I've seen manuscripts that have been through three editors and multiple beta readers and still have a dozen errors in them, because they started out with so many.

Speech-to-text software has come a long way, but I assume it's still subject to choosing the wrong word and has to be checked over very carefully—even more carefully than if you type directly.

Some of the most common typos to check for are:

- an/and

- ever/every

- has/had

- he/her

- her/here

- him/his

- his/this

- I/in/it

- if/of/on/it/is

- in/on

- know/now

- like/lie

- martial/marital (marital arts are quite different from martial arts, or so I would hope)

- me/my

- not/now

- of/off

- on/of

- on/one

- or/of

- our/out

- quiet/quite

- scrape/scrap

- the/then/them/they

- the/he

- then/than

- thing/think

- though/thought

- to/too

- was/as

- we'll/well

- where/were

- you/your

- missing closing quotation mark (missing the opening mark is less common, but does happen)

- missing period

- missing words, including: to, is/was/be, not, and, the/a/an, had, with, it, of (you can see the pattern, I think: small words that have a mainly grammatical role in the sentence)

The Perils of Revision

IF YOU REVISE A SENTENCE (and you should be revising your sentences), take a few extra moments to check that you've changed everything you need to change and left it in a consistent state, in which it makes sense grammatically and means what you intended.

Check that it still makes sense in its context (the sentences to either side). For example, if you move a sentence that refers to "it", and the object referred to by "it" now occurs in the middle of the previous paragraph (or the next one), you'll need to change "it" to a clearer indication of which object you mean. (The same with "he" and "she", of course.)

Check that you haven't cut out information that you were going to use later on, or, if you have, that you've put it in somewhere else.

If you've switched a name for a pronoun or vice versa, check that you haven't also left the original word, or part of the original phrase, in place. I've seen a few sentences like "~~I turned the it on~~" or "~~I saw him John~~" in published books.

Check that your verbs and nouns agree in number—that you don't have a singular noun with a plural verb, or vice versa. If you list several things, the verb needs to be plural:

> The aardvark and the alligator were walking down Main Street when it happened.

Spotting the Typos

SOME EDITORS CAN TRAIN themselves to see the words that are actually on the page, rather than the ones that they expect to see. This overcomes the natural human tendency to see what we expect and fill in the gaps (like missing words) without even noticing. Fortunately for my own work, but unfortunately for my uninterrupted enjoyment of other people's, I'm one of the people who see what's there, even though I haven't worked full-time as an editor since the mid-1990s.

You, however, probably don't have that skill (going by statistical likelihood). So what are some tricks to ensure that you haven't missed words from your sentences, or messed them up in some other way?

There are a few. They're tedious, but if you know you often make the mistakes, you need to practice them.

1. Read backwards. This makes you see the words one at a time.
2. Read upside-down. I used to do this when I was an editor. I don't see it offered as a tip very often, but it worked for me. I'm a fast reader, and reading upside down slowed me down enough that I could notice the errors instead of gliding past them.If you read on paper or on an e-reader like a Kindle, reading upside down is straightforward, but on a computer screen you may need to output the text to a PDF file and then rotate it in your PDF reading software. Tablets, which usually detect their orientation and show you the text the right way up regardless of how you turn them, can be set not to do that (this also applies to some brands of e-reader). Google will tell you how to do it for your particular device.

3. Read aloud. Again, this slows you down, and also highlights issues with your sentence structure, unintended verbal patterns which will distract your readers, sentences that are too long, and the need for more or different punctuation. Also, if you ever intend to have an audio version of your book, it needs to work in that medium. Reading it aloud is a good way to check whether it does.This won't help you with homonym errors (words that sound the same), but it will help with missing words.

4. Have someone else read it aloud, if you have someone who will do so.

5. Have a device read it to you using text-to-speech. Windows 7+, Mac OS X+, iOS 8+, and Android since early versions have built-in text-to-speech (Google "text to speech" and the name of your operating system to find out how to enable this on each platform). There are also free applications for all the platforms which will do text-to-speech with varying degrees of usability and pleasantness. Some older e-ink Kindles, and of course the Kindle tablets, have text-to-speech capability. So does Scrivener, the popular writing software (http://literatureandlatte.com), under the Edit > Speech menu.Paid apps exist too, of course, which may or may not be superior. Read some reviews and make your choice. I can't provide a lot of guidance, since I haven't used this approach myself, but if you often miss words out of sentences or make simple typos that can be detected by listening, it's likely to help you.

6. Proofread on an e-reader. I find that I spot more typos on my e-reader than I do when I read a print book, and I suspect it's because there are fewer words to a line.Most e-readers will provide a way to "side-load" content. Consult

Google about how to get your book's draft onto your e-reader of choice.

WHATEVER TOOL YOU USE for writing (Word, Google Docs, Scrivener) should have a built-in spellcheck. Pay attention to it. I've seen several published books, including at least one from a major publisher (*cough*HarperCollins*cough*), which included errors that a simple spellcheck should have caught.

Google Docs is also surprisingly good at spotting typos, probably using some of the knowledge built up by its search tool ("Did you mean to search for...?"). Still, only trust Google Docs' advice if you're sure it's correct—it's a reminder, not a tutor. (It also suggests "alright" for "all right," which I, and the major style guides, still consider incorrect, though that fight will probably be lost in the long term; see my discussion below, Is "alright" all right?)

MS Word's grammar checker is wrong far more often than it's right. For example, shown the sentence above that includes "if you're sure it's correct", it incorrectly suggests "its" for "it's". Even when it's right, it's oriented to business writing, not fiction. It should be ignored with extreme prejudice.

And, at the time of writing, there's a significant fault with Apple's autocorrect which makes it auto-incorrect. If you write a piece of dialog ending with a question mark or exclamation mark, close the quotation mark, and add a tag such as "he asked," it will turn the first letter of the tag into a capital, as if it was starting a new sentence. This is not correct (see Punctuating Dialog), and you should find the setting on your Apple device, if you use one to write, and turn it off.

Chapter 2: Apostrophes

People often get apostrophes wrong in written English.

Apostrophes actually follow two simple rules, even if one of them is slightly confusing (as we'll discuss below). Here are the rules:

1. *An apostrophe is used after a noun to indicate that the person or thing referred to by the noun owns something. If an "s" is pronounced, and isn't already part of the noun, it goes after the apostrophe.*
2. *An apostrophe is used to indicate that one or more letters have been left out of a word in the speaker's pronunciation.*

Some people who are under the vague impression that apostrophes occur before the letter "s" at the end of words will add apostrophes where they don't belong. This is called the "greengrocer's apostrophe," because you often see it outside the business premises of people who think they are selling **"~~potatoe's~~". They aren't. They are selling potatoes. Nor do you need an apostrophe in the expression "the ones responsible," or in the name of a decade, like "the 1960s," or in the plural of an abbreviation, like "AIs" (even though, in that case, letters have been left out). Older practice sometimes inserted apostrophes after decades or abbreviations, but you should leave them out so that it's clear when the word is plural and when it's possessive.

Let's look at both of the apostrophe rules, break them down and explain some of the ways in which people (even good writers) get confused about them.

If you're not familiar, or not confident, with the terminology of nouns and pronouns, I suggest reviewing that section before you read this one, because it assumes you know what a noun is and what a pronoun is.

1. Possessive Apostrophes

———

Here's our first rule again:

An apostrophe is used after a noun to indicate that the person or thing referred to by the noun owns something. If an "s" is pronounced, and isn't already part of the noun, it goes after the apostrophe.

The straightforward case first: singular noun (only one person or thing).

The alligator belongs to John. It is *John's* alligator.

Please forgive me for beginning with the very basics. People do still get this one wrong, leaving the apostrophe out or putting it in the wrong place. Most of them aren't writers, but a few are.

That was simple. How about a plural noun? The rule again: The apostrophe goes after the noun. If an "s" is pronounced, and it isn't already part of the noun, it goes after the apostrophe. So the order is: noun, apostrophe, extra "s" if needed.

The entrance is used by the servants. It is the *servants'* entrance.

That's one that a surprisingly large number of writers get wrong, even writers who otherwise make few errors. All the servants, not just one servant, own (or use) the entrance, so "servants" is the noun. After that comes the apostrophe. There's already an "s," so we don't need another one. Similarly, the merchants' quarter, the apothecaries' guild; more than one merchant or apothecary is involved, so the apostrophe goes after the s.

I read a book once that referred to "the Peasant's Revolt". Poor fellow, he can't have got very far by himself.

A very common error along these lines is to write ***"~~my parent's house~~" when you mean the house belonging to both parents. The correct punctuation is, as you can probably work out by now, "my parents' house".

There is what looks like an exception, but really isn't, to the rule I've just outlined. If you're referring to clothing or other equipment, it's considered correct to write a sentence like "He wore wizard's robes." By extension from this, it can also be considered correct to say, "They all wore soldier's uniforms." Even though there were multiple people wearing multiple uniforms, each of them individually wore a soldier's uniform, I suppose is the logic—though looking for logic in English usage is a bit like looking for honesty among politicians; sometimes you'll find some, but it's always a surprise.

Now, there are a few nouns in English (*men, women, children, brethren* and *oxen*) that preserve an old-fashioned plural form from before everything else standardised on the "s" plural. I've seen people get possessive apostrophes wrong with these because they don't know the rule properly, or don't think it through.

> The aardvark belongs to the children. It is the *children's* aardvark.

Resist the temptation to put the apostrophe after the "s", and think through the rule. Noun, apostrophe, then "s" if it's needed. "Children" is the noun, so the apostrophe goes straight after it, and then the "s" at the end. Likewise "men's" and "women's".

Another one to watch for: "people's". The noun is *people*. It's already implicitly plural. The apostrophe goes after it, and then the "s"—unless the noun itself is "peoples," in a sentence like this:

> These ancient *peoples'* migratory tracks formed the basis of modern highways.

In that case, we are using "peoples" in the sense of "groups of people" or "tribes". See Unusual Plurals.

"Others" is another tricky one. Be careful about the rule:

> They looked into *each other's* eyes.

> The *others'* faces held a shocked expression.

Both those sentences are right, because in the first case the base noun is "each other," and in the second case it's "the others".

What about if you're talking about a family, using their surname to refer to them collectively? Same rule: noun (which is the family's name, but in the plural form because you're talking about more than one of them), apostrophe, extra "s" if you pronounce one—but you don't, because it's already part of the noun.

> This archaeological dig belongs to the Joneses. It is the *Joneses'* archaeological dig.

> This spaceship belongs to the Robinsons. It is the *Robinsons'* spaceship.

But if you're using an individual's surname, you do put an extra "s" after the apostrophe, if you pronounce it:

> This is *Indiana Jones's* dig.

This is *Tom Robinson's* spaceship.

Some people don't pronounce the extra "s" if there's already one in the name:

This is *Ezekiel Jones'* desk.

Either way, the rule works.

If the family name ends in "s," don't put the apostrophe before it:

~~**The Jenkins family is well known hereabouts. This is Fred Jenkin's boy.~~

That one rule is all you need to know to get possessive plurals right 100% of the time. Noun (singular or plural), then the apostrophe, and finally another "s" if you pronounce it and it isn't already part of the noun.

Pronouns don't count as nouns for purposes of this rule, by the way. I'll talk about them more below.

2. Abbreviating Apostrophes

Apostrophes also have another purpose, as in our second rule:

An apostrophe is used to indicate that one or more letters have been left out of a word in the speaker's pronunciation.

For example: isn't, ain't, don't, let's, we'll, you'd, hangin', 'Arry.

In the case of *isn't*, *ain't* and *don't*, the missing letter is the "o" of "not".

In the case of *let's*, the missing letter is the "u" of "us".

It isn't always just one letter. In the case of *we'll*, there are two missing letters, the "w" and "i" of "will". The word *you'd* drops almost the whole of the word "would," four out of the five letters.

Notice that all of these are examples where two words have been compressed into one. The missing space just goes missing, with no apostrophe to mark its disappearance. It gets no respect.

The missing letter or letters can be at the beginning or end of the word, as well as in the middle, as in *hangin'* or *'Arry* (Harry pronounced with a Cockney accent - notice that the A takes over the capital, because it's someone's name).

As a side note, use this kind of dialect indicator sparingly. It quickly becomes annoying to the reader, and it marks the speaker's dialect as "non-standard" and subtly implies that he or she is therefore inferior to speakers of "standard" English. There's a long-standing convention that main characters don't speak dialect, even if every character around them who comes from the same background does, because dialect is alienating to the reader. Think twice about drawing attention to your characters' pronunciation in this way (though a few carefully chosen, and *correctly used*, dialect phrasings or words can be appropriate to strengthen a character's voice).

So What About Pronouns?

THE MOST COMMON APOSTROPHE mistakes by far are the ones with pronouns, like it's/its, they're/their and so forth. This is for a couple of reasons.

The first is that our minds don't always clearly distinguish between two words that sound alike but are spelled differently. It's a glitch in our mental software. Even if you know which word is the right one, you may sometimes type the wrong one, especially if you're in a hurry or distracted. If you know you're prone to doing that, you need to become more vigilant in checking your work. (See my tips for catching more typos.)

The second reason people confuse these words is that they are confusing. It seems like the first rule should apply, and *it's* should mean "belonging to it". But actually the second rule applies, and *it's* means *it is*.

If it helps, you can think of it this way: pronouns (*it*, *they* and so forth) don't count as full nouns, and so don't share in their privileges or responsibilities when it comes to apostrophe rule number one.

What may help more is my simple trick for keeping these pairs of words straight. Just compare them to *she's* and *her*, which sound completely different from each other, but follow the same pattern as the rest of the pronouns. Like this:

Pronoun	[Pronoun] is	Belonging to [Pronoun]
she	she's	her
he	he's	his
it	it's	its
they	they're	their
we	we're	our
who	who's	whose

If you're genuinely stuck and can't remember which way round the rule goes, ask yourself "would I say *she's* or *her* if I was talking about a woman here?" Then use the form with the same number of apostrophes.

We've already talked about typos like *we're/were* and *we'll/well* previously. Those are usually problems of the typing hands more than problems of understanding.

I hope that's made the rules of apostrophes clearer for you.

Special Phrases and Special Cases

There are a few phrases that require apostrophes but don't always get them, or get them when they shouldn't. Again, if you think them through you'll understand why the apostrophe should or should not be there.

One is *arm's length*, as in "she kept him at arm's length". It means that she kept him at the length of her arm—or, if you like, at the length belonging to her arm. You could make a case for phrasing it as *at arms' length*, meaning at the length of (both her) arms, though that isn't how it's most commonly punctuated. In either case, the apostrophe still needs to be in there.

Similarly, *at his wits' end* (the end of his wits, not the end of his wit), *for goodness' sake* (for the sake of goodness), and *for old times' sake* (for the sake of old times, not old time).

On the other hand, *for all it's worth* means "for all it is worth", not "for all the worth of it." Either one would make sense in this case, but the first is the usual meaning and usage.

Another phrase people get wrong is *old wives' tale*. That should be self-explanatory by now.

And then there's *three weeks' notice*. I often see variations of this (with various lengths of time) missing their apostrophe. It's not instantly obvious that the apostrophe is needed, but think for a moment: you'd say *a week's notice*, not ~~a week notice~~. If it's *a week's notice* then it needs to be *three weeks' notice* to be consistent and follow our first rule. *Ten dollars' worth* is the same pattern.

Missing persons case doesn't have an apostrophe. Apparently it's plural, even if only one person is missing. Same with *weapons fire* and *arms race*.

Likewise *first things first*. We're talking about more than one thing, and the things don't own anything, nor are we saying "(the) first thing is first".

Likewise *heads up* and *thumbs up* and *hats off* ("hats off to Larry!").

Rephrasing for Clarity and Smoothness

SOMETIMES YOU NEED to rephrase in order to make a sentence less awkward:

> **He grabbed the taller of his sons' arm.**

Although that's technically correct, this reads better:

> He grabbed the arm of the taller of his sons.

Any time you have several people with various limbs, possessions, etc. in your sentence, and you're making a generalisation or distinction about those possessions, you need to watch your phrasing to make sure it's totally clear and not horribly awkward.

Here's another crying out for a rephrase:

> between one of his goat's ears

Not only is the apostrophe in the wrong place, since the man in question has several goats, but even if it was in the right place it would be awkward. Rephrase:

> between the ears of one of his goats

Another unusual case where rephrasing would help: where a name (such as the name of a business) already has an apostrophe in its normal spelling. I'll use Mulcahy's, which is a bar in one of my own series, as an example, though I have in mind another writer's work.

Rather than:

> ~~I opened Mulcahy's door.~~

Try:

> I opened the door of Mulcahy's.

The reason is that the door belongs to Mulcahy's, not to Mulcahy (who may be fictional, or deceased, or have sold the business years ago). Therefore, according to our Possessive Apostrophes rule above (take what owns the thing, add an apostrophe, add another "s" if it's pronounced), the punctuation should be ~~Mulcahy's'~~, but that's ridiculous. Much better to rephrase.

See also Clarity of Reference.

Chapter 3: Narrative Tense

If you're not familiar with the terminology of verbs, review the section on verbs later in the book before reading this section.

Past, Present, and Perfect Tense

M ost fiction is narrated in the past tense: *This happened, then that happened.* You're telling the story afterwards, which is how we usually tell stories. It is possible to write it in present tense (*this happens, that happens*), and some people like the immediacy that brings, but it's a tense that draws attention to itself because it isn't the default choice. That can make it sound pretentious, especially if there's no particular reason to use it. (There's also a risk that you'll slip and fall into past tense occasionally without meaning to, something I've seen happen in several long present-tense narratives.)

Assuming you're picking the default and narrating in the past tense, in a sense the past becomes the story's "present". The time being described in the main narrative is the moving moment in which the action is taking place—a moment that existed in the past. Whether it's yesterday, last week, or a thousand years ago, there's a particular time when the action you're describing occurred. So what happens when you need to refer back to something that happened *before* that moving moment?

Increasingly often (based on the books I read), inexperienced writers make no distinction. They just narrate the earlier event in the same past tense as the main action.

Just as poorly handled "blocking" (the visualisation and description of locations and movement in space) will confuse your readers because they can't imagine *where* things happened, poorly handled tense will confuse them because it isn't clear *when* things happened.

There's a tool for that, and it's called the **past perfect**.

You can think of the past perfect as the "past of the past" if it makes it easier (or not, if it doesn't). The key word that makes past perfect work is "had". This signals to the reader that we've left the moment of the action and moved to an earlier time. When the "had" sentences stop and we come back to the simple past, that signals the end of the flashback or summary of earlier events. We've now returned to the main flow of the narrative.

It works like this:

> John knew how to use the past perfect tense, because one of his professors had taught it to him.

At the narrative moment, John knew a skill. Prior to the narrative moment, one of his professors *had taught* it to him; the professor was not teaching him at the narrative moment. By using "had", I signal the reader that the teaching happened prior to the time that the main action took place. It's confusing to say:

> ~~John knew how to use the past perfect tense, because one of his professors taught it to him.~~

The teaching happened before the knowing.

Now, that example isn't necessarily all that confusing. An alert reader will figure out that the teaching happened before the knowing without too much of a blip. But people who have a habit of leaving out the past perfect frequently do confuse their readers, when they switch, without signalling, from talking about the moment of the present action to talking about earlier events. Consider this sentence:

> ~~The implications of what she did struck him.~~

If "what she did" was a thing that happened at a previous time, say, the day before or the week before, this is disorienting to the reader, who is whiplashed from the previous week to the current narrative moment without notice. In the particular example I'm paraphrasing there, "she" wasn't even present in the scene, which made it still more disorienting. Much better and clearer to say:

> The implications of what she had done struck him.

Sometimes, using the past perfect tense correctly will require you to type "had had":

> I had had too much ice cream and was feeling unwell.

There's nothing wrong with that, though some word processing programs will question the repeated word. Ignore them.

Here's another example, slightly altered to disguise its origin (in a book I reviewed):

> ~~***Thomas presented us with the small black case I saw him carry in.~~

The narrator saw Thomas carry the case in when they arrived in the room, and he presented it some time afterwards, but you wouldn't immediately know that from this sentence. It would be much clearer if the author wrote:

> Thomas presented us with the small black case I had seen him carry in.

The same author has a habit of using "you've" ("you have") where she means "you'd" ("you had"). This puts us momentarily into the present tense instead of the past, and again confuses the reader.

Another example from a different author:

~~***Peter assured Edward that he made improvements.~~

This should be:

Peter assured Edward that he had made improvements.

The improvements had already been made in the past at the time that Peter and Edward had the conversation. If you say "he made improvements," that means it was Peter's habit or occupation to make improvements, that he did it constantly or regularly, rather than that he had done so at a specific time in the past.

These ones are from a writer who was nominated for a prestigious award, in a book published by one of the largest publishers in the world (just so you know how common it is to make these errors):

~~***He quit years ago.~~

~~***If I arrived earlier, I would have been too tired to help.~~

Clearer versions would have been:

He had quit years ago.

If I had arrived earlier, I would have been too tired to help.

Here's another, from a different writer:

~~***She took on so many of her mother's domestic duties in the three years since losing her.~~

Try:

She had taken on so many of her mother's domestic duties in the three years since losing her.

And another writer:

> **~~There was a chance my mother locked it when she'd gone to bed.~~

That one creates, if anything, worse confusion by starting out in simple past and not hitting the past perfect until the end of the sentence, while it should have come in the middle:

> There was a chance my mother had locked it when she'd gone to bed.

Once you have established the past perfect, you don't need to keep using it constantly. This version of the sentence is also perfectly fine:

> There was a chance my mother had locked it when she went to bed.

The "had" signals that the locking took place in the "past of the past," not in the story's narrative moment. Once you make that clear, you can keep going in the simple past. It can be a good idea to use another "had" (or whatever grammatical variation of "had" fits your sentence) to bookend the mini-flashback before you come back into the original narrative moment:

> There was a chance my mother had locked it when she went to bed. It would be like her to have done so, I reflected.

Using the past perfect is important when you're indicating a change in perspective from past to present. For example:

~~This was the last thing she expected.~~

It was the last thing she *had* expected, but now that she was seeing it, her perspective had presumably changed. Likewise:

~~She had no idea how valuable that watch had been.~~

She *had* had no idea, but now she realized the value of the watch.

Also:

~~She realized there was never anything to fear.~~

She realized there *had never been* anything to fear.

The same author who wrote those sentences also had a tendency to write sentences to this pattern:

~~She started to ascend when a small red light caught her eye.~~

Based on the grammar of the sentence, the plain meaning is that a small red light caught her eye and then somehow triggered the start of her ascent. This would be bad writing if that was what the author meant, since it's describing the effect before the cause. But what she actually meant was:

She *had* started to ascend when a small red light caught her eye.

This is in the correct chronological order, and makes it clear that the two things (her action of starting to ascend and the light catching her eye) were not connected in a cause-and-effect relationship, but just two things that happened close together in time, and in a particular order.

I've also seen the past perfect tense used when it should be simple perfect, because the event referred to occurred in the same timeframe as the current narrative.

For example, I've seen the phrase "it might not have been as grand" used when the thing referred to was still grand at the narrative moment; the phrasing should have been "it might not be as grand".

Just as clear signalling when you manoeuvre on the road lets your fellow drivers know where you're going, so clear signalling with your tenses lets your reader know, without having to puzzle it out, what the sequence of events was.

There's a **present perfect** as well as a past perfect tense. It indicates that the action of the main verb is already completed at the present moment, and it uses the present tense of the verb "to have" instead of the past tense as its signal:

> I have learned how to use present perfect tense.

> John has known how to use present perfect tense for years.

Make sure that you keep past perfect and present perfect straight. It's very easy to mistype "has" for "had" or vice versa, for example.

Use "had" if you are narrating in past tense and referring to something that finished happening before the narrative moment.

Use "has" if you are narrating in present tense and referring to something that finished happening before the present (which is your narrative moment).

There's a pitfall with the perfect tenses that I've seen a few people fall into. The perfect tenses (and the passive voice) put the main verb in the form that's known as the *past participle*. Most often, this is the same as the simple past tense, but for irregular verbs (ones that signal past tense in some other way than adding -ed at the end), it isn't.

So:

> I constructed a building.

> I should have constructed a building.

but:

> I wrote a book.

> I should *have written* a book.

I've seen the second of those incorrectly rendered this way:

> ~~I should have wrote a book.~~

As with anything, if you're representing someone's dialect (someone from the southern US or blue-collar New York City, for example) and that is how they talk, by all means use it, but avoid it in narration if you're going for a neutral voice; it will stand out as an error.

May or Might ?

———

Another common error is also about past-tense narration, so I'll talk about it next.

Consider these sentences:

> I **know** that I **can** use tense correctly.
>
> I **knew** that I **could** use tense correctly.
>
> I **say** that I **will** use tense correctly.
>
> I **said** that I **would** use tense correctly.
>
> I **hope** that I **may** use tense correctly.
>
> I **hoped** that I **might** use tense correctly.

Note that last one in particular. Surprisingly often, I see an author narrating in the past tense use "may" rather than "might". I don't know why people don't get "can/could" and "will/would" wrong, but do get "may/might" wrong. (I have actually seen a couple of authors get "will/would" wrong, but only a couple).

It is wrong, though. There's a narrative convention known as "free indirect speech," which is a summary of what someone said or thought, rather than a quotation or transcription of their exact words or thoughts. All of the above examples are in free indirect speech, and when you're using free indirect speech in a past-tense narrative, the speech gets converted into the past tense as well. *All* of the speech, including "may" being converted to "might".

"May" and "might" do have some differences in usage, and they're used sometimes to mean subtly different things, but in the case of free indirect speech, convert "may" to "might". Otherwise, the effect is as if your past tense narration switched momentarily into the present. It draws attention to itself, and can cause readers to stumble.

"May" signals a situation that's still continuing, and suggests present tense, so unless you want to signal that your hypothetical situation still exists, use "might" with past tense narration. For example:

> ***~~It may pain him if I were killed~~.

This is out of place in past tense narration. It should be:

> It might pain him if I were killed.

Here's a made-up example which may help to make it clearer (I just said "may" because I'm talking to you in the present):

> ***~~The British may not consider Napoleon a threat at this point, but they still assigned Rogier to spy on him.~~

> The British might not consider Napoleon a threat at this point, but they still assigned Rogier to spy on him.

The first version brings us into the present and implies that the British could (but don't) consider Napoleon a threat today, and that their assignment of a spy two hundred years ago is somehow related to this, which is absurd. The second version keeps us in the past throughout.

Oddly enough, I haven't noticed the same issue with "can" and "could," a similar pair of words, except once, from an author whose first language wasn't English.

"May" and "might" can also convey entirely different meanings, quite apart from the tense issue. An acquaintance of mine wrote a social media post which linked to an article about a dangerous driver and remarked "she may have killed someone". This led me to the conclusion that someone was lying in a hospital, possibly dying, because of this woman. When I read the article, though, she hadn't killed anyone, and there was no suspicion that she had. What he meant was "she might have killed someone" (it could have happened, given her behaviour, but it didn't). Saying "she may have killed someone" suggests that the question hasn't been resolved yet; we don't know if she did or not.

Most may/might confusions aren't this dramatic. It's still worth bearing in mind that using "may" in the middle of a past tense narrative brings us, effectively, into the present tense.

Is or Was?

I also see authors occasionally struggling with when to use "is" versus "was" in past tense narration. The simple rule is: If you're narrating in the past tense and describing a state of affairs that outlasts the narrative moment because it's essentially permanent, use "is". Otherwise, keep your narrative tense consistent and use "was".

Examples:

He knew that Norway **is** located in northern Europe.

That's in present tense, even though the sentence is in the past tense, because it's a fact that not only is still true, but will continue to be true as long as Norway exists. However:

He knew that Norway **was** ruled by King Harald V.

Facts of this type, which are more time-bound than the geographical location of Norway, should be narrated in the same tense as the narrative itself—in this case, the past tense—even if, at the time of writing, they are still true.

In the case of a story set outside our world's history, or even inside our world's history where it's not clear exactly when the story is being told, use "was" for anything except a fact of the first type that is unlikely to ever change.

Chapter 4: Commas of Identity

I've invented the term "commas of identity" to cover two errors I often see from inexperienced writers and, in the second case, from journalists, who are often not given any training in basic writing mechanics. Both of them relate to people's identities.

The Vocative Comma: Let's Eat Grandma!

"Vocative" just means that you're addressing someone, so the "vocative comma" is the comma you use when you're addressing someone—whether by their name, their title, or some other form of address.

Consider these sentences:

I don't know, Jack.

I don't know Jack.

Let's eat, Grandma!

Let's eat Grandma!

Call me, Ishmael.

Call me Ishmael.

Wake up, Daddy.

Wake up Daddy.

The first in each pair uses the vocative comma, and addresses Jack, Grandma, Ishmael and Daddy. The second in each pair doesn't, and it means something different. Instead of being addressed, Jack, Grandma, Ishmael and Daddy are the objects of those sentences, and are (as grammarians say) suffering the action of the verb. Grandma is suffering rather more literally than the others.

The first example ("I don't know Jack") means that I'm not acquainted with Jack, or, colloquially, that I don't know anything (though that wouldn't usually require a capital J).

The third example ("Call me Ishmael") instructs the hearer to address the speaker by the name Ishmael, and is, of course, the famous first line of *Moby Dick*, whereas "Call me, Ishmael" addresses Ishmael and instructs him to call the speaker.

I also saw (not in a book) a report of a wedding invitation that said "No white ladies." The intention was to alert female guests to the dress code, that only the bride should wear white. The actual message delivered... was different. Likewise with a bumper sticker that says "Shoot straight boys."

The vocative comma is *always* required, any time someone is being addressed. This is true whether the term of address is at the start of the sentence:

> Mr. Watson, come here—I want to see you.

In the middle of the sentence:

> I have to say, Colonel Baird, that's remarkable.

Or at the end of the sentence:

> What a day, bro.

The vocative comma comes after a term of address at the beginning; before and after a term of address in the middle; and before a term of address at the end.

If you leave the vocative comma out, not only do you risk suggesting to your family that you should cannibalize your grandmother, but your sentences will sound breathless and rushed. You can use it deliberately to create that effect, of course—I've done so—but in general, show your readers that you know the rule (and keep your sentences unambiguous) by putting in the commas. Leaving them out is one of the mistakes that, to me, most clearly distinguishes professional from unprofessional writing.

Always, without exception, use a comma before a term of address in dialog, also:

> "Fascinating, Captain."

> "I want to get to know you better, John."

This rule only applies to terms of address, though:

> "I'm fascinated by the captain."

> "I want to get to know John better."

In those examples, you're talking about the person, not to them, so there's no comma.

Always use a comma after a term of address, as well:

> "John, come and look at this aardvark."

> "Captain, I canna give ye any more power!"

And if the term of address comes in the middle of a sentence, it gets commas both before and after:

> "Dammit, Jim, I'm a doctor, not a grammarian!"

The Appositive Comma

Before I talk about the appositive comma, I need to lay some groundwork.

Noun phrases are multi-word phrases which, at a high level of sentence analysis, act like nouns (for purposes of deciding where a comma goes, for example). Noun phrases can have internal grammatical structure, but as a whole they can be substituted for a simple noun in the same grammatical role:

> John ate the cheeseburger.

> The Bishop of Winton and Emeritus Professor of Consequential Studies at the University of Colby ate the cheeseburger.

Both of those sentences are, at a high level, grammatically identical: they consist of a subject (the noun that does the action), a verb (the action), and an object (the noun that has the action done to it). In the first example, the subject is "John". In the second, it is "The Bishop of Winton and Emeritus Professor of Consequential Studies at the University of Colby," who may or may not be the same person as "John". The verb in both cases is "ate," and the object in both cases is "the cheeseburger".

There can be commas within a noun phrase. They go between different descriptions of the same person, place or thing:

> The Bishop of Winton and Emeritus Professor of Consequential Studies at the University of Colby, the Most Reverend Professor Sir John Herbert Frederic

Arthur Lamington IV, who looks to the left and to the right and whose titles grow ever more lengthy, ate the cheeseburger.

This kind of construction is the only time that you need a comma between the subject and the main verb ("ate" in this case). The comma in question is *the second of a pair*, which sets off one of the alternative noun phrases from the others. (All three of those noun phrases describe the same person.) The commas act like a parenthesis: ( ). You could substitute a pair of dashes; the main point to grasp here is that they are a pair of punctuation marks, enclosing the phrase and setting it off as separate. I've seen far too many examples where someone with a vague grasp of comma usage puts a single unpaired comma before the main verb.

Historical note: in 19th-century and early-20th-century English, authors such as Charles Dickens did sometimes put a single comma before the main verb, usually when they had started out with a complicated multi-word phrase before reaching the verb. The intention may well have been to signal the end of the complicated phrase. This is no longer considered correct, and writing like this is also out of fashion.

Constructions between pairs of commas like the above are a specific kind of parenthesis called an **appositive** (thanks to Grammar Girl Mignon Fogarty for teaching me this: http://www.quickanddirtytips.com/education/grammar/ where-do-i-use-commas).

If you read the Grammar Girl article, you'll learn that there are restrictive and non-restrictive forms of appositive, and commas are only required for the nonrestrictive one (where you're directly renaming or redescribing something that you've already named or described). This leads to one of those obscure comma rules that you don't need to worry about too much. It works this way:

> My brother, Roger, lives in Australia.

> My sister Jan lives in Tauranga.

Both of those sentences are correctly punctuated. The reason is that I only have one brother, so "my brother" and "Roger" are the same person (it's a nonrestrictive appositive, a direct renaming). However, I have two sisters, so "Jan" is a restrictive appositive—it clarifies which sister I'm talking about.

Very few people know this rule, so if you mess it up hardly anyone will care (though it's more important when you use it with relative clauses, which we'll talk about below). The important point is this: if you use a name or description for someone or something, and then immediately afterwards use another name or description for the same person or thing, separate them with a comma. More examples:

> You're going to Hogwarts, a famous school of witchcraft and wizardry.

> I spoke today to Henrietta Wibsley, the world's most prominent aardvark.

Use commas if:

- The phrase can be removed completely without changing the high-level structure of the sentence

- The commas could be replaced with dashes or parentheses

- The phrase is giving more information about the same person or thing, rather than distinguishing it from other people or things (more information = more commas).

Relative Clauses

RELATIVE PRONOUNS (*who, whoever, whose, that, which*) introduce relative clauses, which modify a word, phrase or idea in the main clause.

> The man who shot Liberty Valance was the bravest man of all.

Here, the basic sentence is "The man was the bravest man of all." The relative pronoun "who" introduces a relative clause ("who shot Liberty Valance") which modifies "the man" and tells us which man in particular. Other examples:

> This is the house *that* Jack built.

> The man *whose* house it was died.

> The aardvark *of which* I spoke climbed the Matterhorn.

> The place *where* it happened is marked with a stone.

> The time *when* that was acceptable is over.

All of these are **restrictive relative clauses**. The relative clause is distinguishing something from other things of its type: *the man whose house it was* as opposed to other men, *the aardvark of which I spoke* as opposed to other aardvarks. It's restricting the reference to one particular man or aardvark. Restrictive relative clauses don't get commas, just like the restrictive appositives we talked about before under nouns.

There are also *non-restrictive relative clauses*, which do require commas (like non-restrictive appositives). You can tell them from the restrictive ones because, although they do provide extra information, it isn't information that's there to distinguish one object or person from another:

> The house, which he had painted the previous weekend, burned down.

> The aardvark climbed the Matterhorn, which surprised the Swiss.

You can remove the entire non-restrictive relative clause and you still know just as much as you knew before about which house or which aardvark we are discussing.

I saw something like the following sentence in a book once:

> ~~The security guards, who weren't hurrying the shoppers to the exits, hid from the gunman behind the furniture.~~

I'm reasonably sure that the author meant to distinguish one group of security guards (who were hurrying the shoppers to the exits) from another group (who were hiding behind the furniture). However, she mispunctuated the sentence, and it came out meaning that all of the security guards were hiding instead of helping. She made the relative clause non-restrictive instead of restrictive.

As with appositives, use commas with a relative clause if:

- The clause can be removed completely without changing the high-level structure of the sentence

- The commas could be replaced with dashes or parentheses

- The clause is giving more information about the same person or thing, rather than distinguishing it from other people or things (more information = more commas).

A note on "which/who" versus "that". Americans are sometimes taught that "which" (for objects) or "who" (for people) is more correct in formal contexts than "that". British and Commonwealth English considers "that" equally correct.

Also, "that" is fine after all, any, anything, every, everything, few, no, nothing, little, many, much, none, some or something (all of which indicate quantity in some way):

> Every engineer that graduates from this university receives a ring.

Nobody will pull you up for using "who" in this case, though.

Because "that" is sometimes appositive, some people tend to use a comma before it whenever it appears, whether it's appositive or not:

> **I said to her, that I wasn't at all surprised.

Make sure you only place a comma before "that" if it is acting as an appositive.

Chapter 5: Commas of Sequence

Commas of sequence is another phrase I've made up to group together a couple of different issues. The more important issue, because it's the one that I most often see people getting wrong, is the first one. In fact, I see even writers who have otherwise good mechanics getting it wrong.

The Coordinate Comma

The coordinate comma is the comma that sometimes goes between adjectives in a list:

Henrietta was a famous, wealthy aardvark.

You could replace the comma in that sentence with "and":

Henrietta was a famous and wealthy aardvark.

Or you could mix them round:

Henrietta was a wealthy, famous aardvark.

Neither of those adjectives sticks more strongly to "aardvark" than the other. But consider this sentence:

Henrietta was a small grey aardvark.

You wouldn't say:

Henrietta was a small and grey aardvark.

Nor would you say:

~~Henrietta was a grey small aardvark.~~

And because of those two tests, you also shouldn't punctuate it like this:

~~Henrietta was a small, grey aardvark.~~

The comma doesn't belong there. In part, this is because "grey aardvark" forms a unit that is more tightly bound than, say, "famous aardvark"; it seems to be a characteristic of colours and substances in English that they bind to their nouns, almost forming noun phrases. Hence, you'd say "a large stone castle" or "a thick red rug" or "long black hair" or "a thin cotton T-shirt," all without the comma. But if you have a couple of colours (a green-eyed, red-haired woman) the comma belongs in between, since you could swap the order or replace the comma with "and".

In the first edition of this book, I said, "This is kind of an obscure rule, and if you don't know it, or if you mess it up occasionally, most people won't notice." That's true—unless you get it wrong *constantly*. I'm thinking of one book I read in which the author was extremely fond of the pattern "adjective adjective noun," and almost always put a comma in between the two adjectives, and was almost always wrong to do so. There were dozens and dozens of them, and any minor mistake repeated often enough becomes a major mistake. It drove me to distraction—distraction from the story, that is.

Not to mention that she did it in situations like:

~~one, sudden lunge~~

Yes, "one" is technically an adjective (like all numbers). No, you shouldn't put a comma between it and another adjective, because you wouldn't say:

~~sudden, one lunge~~

She also managed to write "~~regular, twenty-second intervals~~", "~~the prevalent, ammonia tang of fish~~", "~~his hated, human shape~~", and "~~black, drawstring trousers~~".

Adjective Sequence

HERE'S ANOTHER WAY to think about it. You may have come across advice somewhere or other that says that adjectives in English always follow the same sequence: number-opinion-size-age-shape-colour-origin-material-purpose:

Six beautiful big old square green French wooden drying racks.

Like most "rules" of English, it isn't completely true in every case, and parts of it are stricter than other parts. You can say "big beautiful field" or "beautiful big field," depending on which quality you want to emphasize, for example, demonstrating that opinion and size can go in either order, even if opinion usually comes first. But you're much more likely to find an opinion adjective before a colour adjective than the other way around:

a beautiful red dress.

Likewise, colour before material is a good rule of thumb:

a grey stone wall.

Because these adjectives of different types occur in a predictable order (I'll say "predictable" rather than "fixed," because English resists being tied down), **they will not have commas between them according to the coordinate comma rule**, which states that you only insert the commas between adjectives if you could switch the order you have them in without it sounding weird. They are *cumulative* adjectives rather than *coordinate* adjectives.

A further implication of this guideline is that if you have two of the same type of adjective—say, two opinions—you can change the order of them freely, and that means they should have commas between them (they are coordinate):

A beautiful, flattering red dress.

A flattering, beautiful red dress.

Note that quantity adjectives—numbers, and general indications of quantity like "some" or "many" or "whole" or "half" or "several"—come even before opinions, which is the usual starting point of most people's lists:

several delicious pizzas

a single beautiful star

a thousand natural shocks

The order of quantity adjectives is, if anything, more fixed than any of the other types; it's very rare indeed to put any adjective before the quantity (I can't think of an example, but with English I don't want to state unequivocally that it never happens). I also can't think of a circumstance in which you'd use two quantity adjectives at the same time; a thing can't have two quantities at once. This means that **you should not put a comma after your quantity adjective, because it will not be coordinate**. A comma after a quantity adjective is one of the most jarring breaches of the coordinate comma rule:

a thousand, tragic shocks

several, delicious pizzas

a single, terrible event

They were just two, scared, homeless kids.

I suspect the author of that last example knew that "two" counted as an adjective but didn't know the rule for when not to use the comma. Because "two" only belongs in that position in that list of adjectives (you wouldn't say "~~scared, two, homeless kids~~"), it doesn't get a comma after it. The comma between "scared" and "homeless" is fine, though, because you could put those adjectives in either order.

A comma after the quantity adjective will look wrong even to people who won't notice other coordinate comma mistakes.

Here's a mnemonic for the list: NO SASh COMP (Number, Opinion, Size, Age, Shape, Colour, Origin, Material, Purpose). I've distinguished size from shape by including the "h" of "shape" in the mnemonic. There are two words that start with O, but if you remember that opinion comes early and origin comes late, you should be covered. Or you could change "NO" to "NOp(e)".

If you are going to use the "adjective adjective noun" pattern often, make sure you learn the coordinate comma rule—*all* of it, not just the "include a comma" part, but the "here's when not to include a comma" part.

There are other mistakes you can make around commas and adjectives. For example, I've seen several authors do this:

> ~~Henrietta was a small, grey, aardvark.~~

In some cases this is because you originally had three adjectives and have taken out the third one, but left the comma after the second. But I know at least one author who has this bad habit of consistently placing an unnecessary and incorrect comma between the last adjective in a list and its noun.

I've even seen this:

> ~~*Her husband's, clean, deep voice~~

Quite apart from the typo "clean" for "clear," that first comma has no business there.

Now and then, the comma can actually change the meaning:

> *Much of their mythology came from long, distant encounters with wizards.

What the author meant was "long-distant encounters," (encounters which were long-distant, or very far away), which is quite different from "long, distant encounters" (encounters which were both long and distant). Actually, what he *really* meant was "long-ago encounters," but that's a different issue.

Commas in Lists

C ommas are also used to separate items in lists:

I bought celery, capers, and aardvark treats.

What I've just demonstrated is called the "Oxford comma," and it's controversial among people who care about commas (who need to get a life, yes, I know). Some say that, since it makes lists less ambiguous sometimes, it should be used all the time. Others disagree.

The Oxford comma is specifically the last comma in the list. Here's a famous example (from an actual newspaper account of a documentary on Merle Haggard):

Among those interviewed were his two ex-wives, Kris Kristofferson and Robert Duvall.

The problem comes because that's a list, but it reads like an appositive (as if "Kris Kristofferson and Robert Duvall" acts as a redescription of "his two ex-wives"). With the Oxford comma, it's clear that it's a list:

Among those interviewed were his two ex-wives, Kris Kristofferson, and Robert Duvall.

In the list "celery, capers and aardvark treats," all three are clearly grocery items, equal members of a list, and so it's just as clear with or without the final comma.

Whether or not to use the Oxford comma is a style choice, unless the sentence is ambiguous without it. If you use it all the time, you won't have to check for ambiguity, and consistency is good too; but make your own decision.

It's still possible to be ambiguous even with the Oxford comma, of course, if something in your list sounds like it could be an appositive for something else. Mignon Fogarty cites[1] "I went to see Zach, an officer, and a gentleman," which could be three people or two (if Zach is an officer). Stay alert to this, and rewrite if necessary. You can represent the three possible meanings of that sentence unambiguously by using different punctuation:

> I went to see Zach—an officer—and a gentleman. (There are two different people: Zach, who is an officer, and someone else, who is a gentleman.)

> I went to see Zach; an officer; and a gentleman. (There are three different people.)

> I went to see Zach—an officer and a gentleman. (There is only one person, Zach, who is also an officer and a gentleman.)

This seems like the place to mention that "and" has a couple of different uses in English. We have been looking at its use in a list, to signal that you've reached the last item in that list, and depending on whether you're using the Oxford comma or not, it may or may not have a comma before it in that usage. It also functions as what's called a "conjunction," though, which I'll talk about more in the chapter on commas of grammatical structure. In this role, it connects two clauses together, and often has a comma before it to indicate the

---

1. http://www.quickanddirtytips.com/education/grammar/serial-comma?page=1

transition point from one clause to the other. The preceding sentence is self-illustrating.

Chapter 6: Commas of Grammatical Structure

When it comes to commas, there are four kinds of author: those who use them correctly; those who use too few (as in the style I call "British breathless," because I see it mostly from UK authors); those who use too many; and those who have about the right number but in the wrong places. I refer to this last kind of author as the "Jackson Pollock," because they litter their manuscripts with commas at random, like paint splashed on a canvas.

Back when I worked as a copy editor for Hodders, there was one author we worked with who, despite having been a senior journalist for many years, had no idea about where to put her commas. We had her under contract for a series of short nonfiction books, unfortunately, and after the first couple of books I started using find-and-replace to strip out all the commas before I even looked at the book, because I knew the vast majority would be in places they didn't belong.

Foolishly, I mentioned to my boss that I was doing this, and—even more foolishly, in my opinion—my boss mentioned it to the author, who threw a fit. I was firmly forbidden from using the nuclear option, and had to go back to removing them one at a time.

There are four kinds of authors, and there are also four kinds of commas. There are commas you must use; commas you must not use; commas you can use if you want; and commas that there's a rule about, but hardly anyone knows the rule, so you'll get away with not following it most of the time.

I won't be talking much about the commas you can use if you want, the ones that you can put in or leave out and still be correct. Whether you use them or not is a matter of style and personal taste, and a way of varying and controlling the pace of your sentences. It'll give your editor something to change if you get everything else right, in order to feel useful.

Much more important are the commas without which your sentences don't flow properly, and the commas which ought not to be inserted.

Commas Not to Use

Do Not Do: Comma Before Main Verb

When I go through a book or story that I'm beta reading and mark errors, a comment I frequently make is "omit comma". Therefore, the kind of comma I want to talk about first is the one which ought not to be inserted.

Notice what I didn't do in that last sentence. I didn't say:

> ***~~The kind of comma I want to talk about first, is the one which ought not to be inserted.~~

This is one of the most common comma errors I see: the excess comma before the main verb. Not only is it not needed, it's incorrect.

From a high-level view, that last example sentence is grammatically the same as this one:

> Henrietta is an aardvark.

"The kind of comma I want to talk about first" is a noun phrase, grammatically equivalent (at a high level) to "Henrietta". There is no justification for separating it from its main verb with a comma. None.

I suspect that the cause of people's confusion on this point is this kind of sentence:

> Henrietta, the person you spoke to yesterday, is an aardvark.

That example does have a comma before the main verb. However, it's the second comma *in a pair*. They're parenthetical commas, and (as "Henrietta is an aardvark" demonstrates), you could lift out everything inside them and the sentence would make sense and be grammatically correct.

You could use dashes instead:

> Henrietta—the person you spoke to yesterday—is an aardvark.

Or parentheses:

> Henrietta (the person you spoke to yesterday) is an aardvark.

For stylistic reasons, to maintain the flow, you'd probably use commas, though.

Note that Dickens, for example, frequently used a comma before a main verb in contravention of this rule, usually after one of his long noun phrases. Dickens was writing well over a century ago, and the rules have changed, and besides, you are not Dickens.

Do Not Do: Comma After Last Adjective

LESS COMMON, BUT STILL something I've seen several authors do, is this:

> ****Henrietta was a small, grey, aardvark.**

See above on commas between adjectives for more discussion.

Do Not Do: Comma in the Middle of a Phrase

HERE'S AN EXAMPLE FROM a published book:

~~*It looked much the same, as the holding cell next door.~~

"Much the same as" is a phrase. Don't insert a comma partway through a phrase.

Do Not Do: Commas Around the Name

HERE'S ANOTHER COMMON comma error that I see, especially from journalists and in the blurbs of indie books:

~~***Prominent aardvark, Henrietta Wibsley, announced today that she would be travelling into space.~~

These commas are unnecessary and incorrect, at least in a sentence phrased this way. I suspect that they've been incorrectly imported from this kind of phrasing:

> The world's most prominent aardvark, Henrietta Wibsley, announced today that she would be travelling into space.

Here, "Henrietta Wibsley" explains who "the world's most prominent aardvark" is. It's an appositive, a parenthetical phrase (explained more fully above). You could also say:

> The world's most prominent aardvark (Henrietta Wibsley) announced today that she would be travelling into space.

In the incorrect example given above, "Prominent aardvark Henrietta Wibsley" is a noun phrase, and shouldn't be broken up by the comma.

The worst example of this error I ever saw was in a blurb for an indie book, which went like this (identifying details altered to protect the guilty):

> *"Meanwhile Pinkerton operatives, Detective, Thomas Wright and, Assistant, Colin..."

Sadly, the rest of the book was just as bad, if not worse, which is a pity, because it also had an original premise and told a good story.

Commas to Use

I mentioned in the introduction to this chapter that some people use too many commas, while others use too few. A piece of writing that's short on commas reads breathlessly, sounds amateurish, and risks confusing the reader by creating ambiguity.

You can get away with few commas if you write mostly short, simple sentences. This puts you in the "spare" or "minimalist" style, though, and the risk is that your writing will sound dull, choppy, simplistic and unsophisticated. If you're aiming for an invisible style (and, again, I urge you to master invisible style before trying anything that draws attention to itself), your average sentence will be medium length—varied with shorter or longer sentences for pacing and impact—and it will require some commas.

In the following, I will talk about dependent and independent clauses. The basic distinction is that a dependent clause cannot function as a sentence by itself, but an independent clause can.

Independent Marker

INDEPENDENT MARKERS LIKE *however* or *therefore* or *in addition* get commas before or after:

> Therefore, I propose that we kill the Batman.

> The aardvark didn't notice, however.

See the section on sentence patterns for more on independent markers.

Dependent Clause at the Beginning of the Sentence

THE BOUNDARY BETWEEN a dependent clause and an independent clause is marked by a comma if the dependent clause comes first:

> While napping, he was stalked by a tiger.

> Waking suddenly, he reached for his gun.

The comma is optional if the dependent clause comes at the end. Again, you'll find more details in the section on sentence patterns about dependent markers.

Minor Clause

IF YOU'RE STARTING or ending your sentence with one or more minor clauses (clauses which could stand on their own as minor sentences—ones without a subject and verb), you need commas to set them off. Likewise if you're stringing a number of them together:

> Listen, um, stay here, OK?

Commas to Use Sometimes

Commas are one of the hardest pieces of punctuation to master, but part of the reason for that, I believe, is that most people don't know the rules—or why they are rules. I hope that, by giving you an outline of grammar and sentence structure, I've helped you to get a better feel for when to use a comma.

Comma usage is sometimes a matter of style, but there are definite places where you must or must not use one, and if you get it wrong, people will notice.

The rest of this section discusses one specialized situation where you might or might not use a comma, depending on what's happening in your sentence.

Of Course There's No Comma

I'VE RECENTLY COME across a few authors who are doing this:

> ***Of course, I am.

They're putting a comma after "of course" whenever it appears. Possibly, they're following the advice of their word processor in doing so (often a bad idea).

As often happens, this tingled my spidey-sense that something was wrong, and then I had to figure out what the rule was.

This is a rare case of grammar that operates across sentence boundaries. If the sentence that begins with "of course" is an answer to another sentence, which is (or can be rephrased as) a question about whether something is or is not the case, it doesn't take the comma:

Are you Henrietta Wibsley?

Of course I am.

The rule operates not only with the "to be" verb, as in the example I just gave, but also with have, do, and the modal verbs (will/would, can/could, may/might, must, shall/should), and where the reply restates the sentence it's responding to:

Does Henrietta know karate?

Of course she does.

Does Henrietta know karate?

Of course she knows karate.

Has Henrietta been into space?

Of course she has.

Will Henrietta be coming?

Of course she will.

Can Henrietta fly a rocket?

Of course she can.

May I sit here?

Of course you may.

Must I salute the general?

Of course you must.

And so on.

The first statement doesn't have to be phrased as a question:

Henrietta can tango.

Of course she can.

There's an implied "can't she?" at the end of the statement.

The rule is actually even simpler than I've stated it above. In all of these cases, the answer could simply be, "Of course." The rest of the sentence is restating or rephrasing part of the question (or original statement). **If the answer could simply be given as "of course," don't use a comma.**

Nor does the phrase have to be "of course"; it can be any equivalent, from "indubitably" to "darn tootin'", from "you bet" to "naturally". I like to think of the late great Alan Rickman in *Harry Potter and the Order of the Phoenix* responding with heavy sarcasm to Dolores Umbridge's rhetorical question about his application to be Defense Against the Dark Arts teacher:

Umbridge: But you were unsuccessful?

Snape: Obviously.

You could expand his answer to "Obviously I was". There's no comma.

So do you ever use a comma with "of course" and its equivalents? Certainly you do. You use it if it's functioning as an independent marker (see above for more on independent markers):

Of course, if you're adding new information that's not a response to the previous sentence, you do need a comma.

You can put the phrase at the end of the sentence that gives new information, of course.

This means, of course, that you can have two versions of the sentence punctuation that are both correct, depending on the sentence that precedes them:

Henrietta is an aardvark. Of course, I knew that.

Did I know that Henrietta was an aardvark? Of course I knew that.

Similarly to the coordinate comma rule, another test for which version applies is whether you can move "of course" to the end without it seeming weird:

Henrietta is an aardvark. I knew that, of course.

~~Did I know that Henrietta was an aardvark? I knew that of course.~~

(Credit to Marie Brennan for pointing out that last test—which does, however, rely on you having good instincts about punctuation in the first place.)

For fiction writing, bear in mind also that the phrase "of course" carries implications about the character who says it and their attitude. It's often used to add authority to a pronouncement that isn't really as certain as the speaker is making out:

Of course, we know exactly why you were there that night.

It's frequently used by academics in this way. There's a bit of unconscious arrogance (and/or conscious bluffing) woven into the usage.

In the non-comma version, responding to a question, it can come across as snippy, carrying the implication "you didn't even need to ask that", or "that's so characteristic for you":

> May I sit here?

> Of course you may.

> I know the answer.

> Of course you do.

It's all in the tone and the relationship, though. "Of course you may sit here" could be kind reassurance to someone lacking in confidence—but it still implies condescension, a superior talking to an inferior.

Some of the equivalent phrases don't necessarily carry this implication. If you ask, "Do you want pizza?" and I respond "Damn straight I do," that's more about being emphatic than being condescending. I'm implying "I am very hungry, and pizza is exactly what I want; thanks for suggesting it."

So, keep in mind the implications of this kind of back-and-forth for the relationships between your characters. But also keep in mind these simple rules:

> *If the sentence is a response to a previous sentence, and could be phrased as simply "of course," don't use a comma after "of course" (or its equivalents).*

If the sentence provides new information that is not a restatement of the previous sentence, use a comma after "of course" at the beginning of the sentence, or before "of course" at the end of the sentence.

Sentence Patterns

Some of the following repeats information in the previous section in a different way, on the principle that explaining it two different ways may increase the number of people who understand it.

There are a number of different possible sentence patterns or structures in English. If you can recognise which pattern you're dealing with, it will be much easier to decide how you should punctuate it.

Varying your sentence patterns will keep your readers from becoming bored. As you increase in skill, you can also use different patterns to shift the emphasis of a sentence, since where you place information in your sentence changes how prominent it is.

Before we get into the patterns, we need some definitions.

The following is partly adapted from material in Purdue University's OWL (Online Writing Lab) at https://owl.english.purdue.edu/owl/[1]. It's an excellent resource, though it's aimed at students writing university papers, rather than at fiction writers, and is incomplete for our purposes.

An **independent clause** can stand on its own as a complete sentence, and expresses a complete thought. It has, as a minimum, a subject (someone or something doing an action) and a verb (the action). It may or may not have an object (someone or something to which the action is done), depending on the verb.

The alligator ate.

---

1. https://owl.english.purdue.edu/owl/section/1/

The alligator ate the aardvark.

An independent clause can (but doesn't have to) begin with an **independent marker word**, such as: *also, consequently, furthermore, however, moreover, nevertheless,* or *therefore.* Look through those words for a minute. Notice what they have in common? They're all to do with putting together a logical sequence of ideas.

A **dependent clause** also has a subject and a verb (and possibly an object), but it is not a complete sentence by itself. If you punctuate it as if it was a sentence, it's called a **sentence fragment**, which is a bad thing. (As usual, dialog is an exception, because folks just talk any old how.)

A dependent clause is often introduced by a **dependent marker word**. Examples include *after, although, as, as if, because, before, even if, even though, if, in order to, since, though, unless, until, whatever, when, whenever, whether,* and *while.*

While the alligator ate the aardvark

Notice what those words have in common? It's a bit more subtle than the independent marker words. Less to do with the abstract, formal logic of ideas and argument, and more to do with how things happen in time; comparing and contrasting; and cause and effect. In other words, you're likely to use a lot more dependent than independent markers in your fiction writing.

The Purdue material states that beginning a clause with one of the seven **coordinating conjunctions** (*and, but, for, or, nor, so,* and *yet*) also signals a dependent clause. However (there's the independent marker word), I disagree. Even if old-fashioned prescriptive grammar says that you can't start a complete sentence with a conjunction, people have been doing it at least since Shakespeare. Also, if you think about it, the difference in meaning between *however* and *but*, or *also* and *and*, or *therefore* and *so* is barely visible to the naked eye. Just because they have more syllables, why should they get more respect?

As we'll see later, there is a difference in punctuation (though that's blurring in practice).

A **minor clause** is the name I'll use for a section of a sentence that could also stand on its own as a **minor sentence**. A minor sentence is one that doesn't have a (fully expressed) subject and a verb, but still works as a complete sentence. Minor sentences include:

- Words or short phrases that can be used as complete answers to questions, like *yes, no, OK, all right, sure.*

- Brief commands or invitations like *listen, come here, shut up, watch out.*

- Interjections like *oh, hey, well, oops, damn.*

In the patterns that follow, anything between square brackets [ ] is required. Anything between curly brackets { } is optional.

Pattern 1: Independent Clause

[INDEPENDENT CLAUSE][.]

Made up of:

[Subject] [Verb] {Object}[.]

An independent clause standing by itself, with no independent marker word, is a **simple sentence**:

John ate.

John ate the cheeseburger.

A simple sentence has simple punctuation. It ends with a period (or a question mark, if it's asked as a question, or an exclamation mark, if it's being exclaimed in dialog—I'll talk more about that in the punctuation chapter).

There are no commas in a simple sentence at its simplest.

Pattern 1a: Independent Clause with Embedded Inessential Information

[SUBJECT][,] [INESSENTIAL clause or phrase][,] [verb] {object}[.]

Now, as we've seen in earlier chapters, a subject which contains a phrase expanding on the noun—a phrase which gives more information about the person or thing—can contain commas, but they're in pairs:

John, who was famous for his gourmet tastes, ate the cheeseburger.

John, the Duke of Brie, ate the cheeseburger.

Everything between the pair of commas can be lifted out of the sentence, and it still makes sense. The commas could be replaced by parentheses or dashes. The added clause or phrase, which is called an appositive, doesn't explicitly distinguish the subject of the sentence from other people or things, it just says more about it.

Apart from these commas (which always come in pairs), *do not place a comma between the subject and the verb*:

~~***John, ate the cheeseburger.~~

Likewise, do not place a comma between the verb and the object:

~~**You can call me, Bill.~~

(That example can be read two ways. The way in which it's incorrectly punctuated is if it means "My name is Bill." It's correctly punctuated if the speaker is talking to Bill and saying that Bill can call the speaker.)

Pattern 1b: Independent Clause with Embedded Essential Information

[SUBJECT] [ESSENTIAL clause or phrase] [verb] {object}[.]

The man who was usually a vegan ate the cheeseburger.

Here, we're explicitly distinguishing this man from other men (we're not just giving additional, inessential information about him). To signal that "the man who was usually a vegan" is a unit, with no extra or inessential information, we leave out the commas.

This sentence could be an answer to the question "Which man ate the cheeseburger?"

Pattern 1c: Independent Clause Introduced with Coordinating Conjunction

[COORDINATING CONJUNCTION] [independent clause][.]

As I said above, I maintain that a sentence beginning with a conjunction is a perfectly cromulent sentence, just as grammatically complete in itself as a sentence beginning with an independent marker word. I'm going against prescriptive grammar in saying that, but I'm in line with long-standing English usage, and since I'm more of a pragmatist than a purist I think that's more important. Here's such a sentence:

> Yet John ate the cheeseburger.

Notice that I haven't put a comma after "yet". I also wouldn't put one after any of the other coordinating conjunctions, like *and, but* or *so.*

Some people do put a comma there, probably because they don't make a distinction from the next pattern. Not every editor will mark this as wrong.

Some LDS writers (notably Brandon Sanderson) often place a comma after initial *but,* for example, which I understand is a stylistic quirk of the Book of Mormon.

Pattern 1d: Independent Clause Introduced with Independent Marker

[INDEPENDENT MARKER][,] [independent clause][.]

> However, John ate the cheeseburger.

If you start your sentence with an independent marker (like *also, therefore* or *nevertheless*), it *must* be followed by a comma. Remember, independent markers are usually related to the logical relationship between ideas.

The following rule of thumb will work most of the time:

- If the introductory word has one syllable, it's probably a coordinating conjunction, so you don't need the comma. Some editors will let you get away with using one.

- If the introductory word has more than one syllable, it's an independent marker, and you do need the comma.

I can think of one exception, *thus*—a one-syllable word which is an independent marker rather than a coordinating conjunction—but how often do you use "thus" in fiction? Seldom, I hope. If you do use it, though, it should be followed by a comma.

Pattern 1e: Independent Clause Followed by Independent Marker

[INDEPENDENT CLAUSE][,] [independent marker][.]

John ate the cheeseburger, however.

The comma is required here as well, just as it is when the independent marker appears at the beginning.

Pattern 1f: Minor Clause Followed by Independent Clause

[MINOR CLAUSE][,] [INDEPENDENT clause][.]

Yes, John ate the cheeseburger.

The comma is required.

You can stack minor clauses, but you need commas between them:

Oh, hey, um, listen, John ate the cheeseburger.

Pattern 1g: Independent Clause Followed by Minor Clause

[INDEPENDENT CLAUSE][,] [minor clause][.]

John ate the cheeseburger, sure.

The comma is required.

Simple sentences are useful, but if you use too many of them in your fiction it will start to sound like a children's book: overly simplistic and sing-song. Let's look at some other sentence patterns.

Pattern 2: Compound Sentence

A COMPOUND SENTENCE consists of two (or more) independent clauses joined together.

If you join them with a comma, you have a comma splice, which is a bad thing. Don't do that.

> ****John ate the cheeseburger, Harry paid for it.**

You can occasionally get away with comma-splicing in informal dialog, where someone is rambling from one idea to the next. But it's better to avoid it.

If you join the independent clauses with no punctuation at all, you have a run-on sentence, which is an even worse thing. Don't do that either, under any circumstances.

> ***John ate the cheeseburger Harry paid for it.**

There are some legitimate ways to form a compound sentence, though.

Pattern 2a: Compound Sentence with Coordinating Conjunction

[INDEPENDENT CLAUSE]{,} [coordinating conjunction] [independent clause][.]

> John ate the cheeseburger, and Harry paid for it.

Or, without the optional comma:

John ate the cheeseburger and Harry paid for it.

The comma is partly stylistic. You can put it in or leave it out as you wish. I would suggest putting it in if either or both of the clauses are long, though, to make it clear where the transition is.

Notice that this isn't the same as:

John ate the cheeseburger and the fries.

That's a simple sentence. The object is *the cheeseburger and the fries.* That's one unit, a noun phrase with no internal punctuation. If you add a comma after "and," the reader will interpret "the fries" as the subject of the second clause, expect the two clauses to have parallel structures, and be confused when the sentence doesn't seem to finish properly by telling you what the fries did:

~~**John ate the cheeseburger, and the fries.~~

If you want to indicate a pause before "and the fries," perhaps for emphasis, you have alternatives:

John ate the cheeseburger—and the fries.

John ate the cheeseburger... and the fries.

John ate the cheeseburger *and* the fries.

Also note that you can't put a comma after the conjunction and be correct:

~~*John ate the cheeseburger, and, Harry paid for it.~~

This is a good argument against using the comma after the conjunction when it starts a sentence.

Pattern 2b: Compound Sentence with Semicolon

[INDEPENDENT CLAUSE][;] [independent clause][.]

John ate the cheeseburger; Harry paid for it.

This pattern is formal, and just a touch pretentious in fiction writing, unless you're going for a ponderous tone or a slight "period" feel. I personally use it too often.

Pattern 2c: Compound Sentence with Semicolon and Independent Marker

[INDEPENDENT CLAUSE][;] [independent marker][,] [independent clause][.]

This is just a combination of Pattern 2b with Pattern 1c.

John ate the cheeseburger; however, Harry paid for it.

Pattern 2d: Compound Sentence with Parallel Structure

THERE IS AT LEAST ONE situation in which you'll get away with joining two independent clauses with a comma: if they have a parallel structure.

[Independent clause][,] [parallel independent clause][.]

John ate the cheeseburger, Harry ate the fries.

An extremely pedantic editor would call that a comma splice, but the fact that both clauses are so similar to each other lets you get away with using just a comma. I'd advise against using this pattern often, though.

Pattern 3: Complex Sentence

A COMPLEX SENTENCE contains an independent clause and at least one dependent clause, often signalled by a dependent marker.

Pattern 3a: Dependent Clause with Dependent Marker at the Beginning

[DEPENDENT MARKER] [dependent clause][,] [independent clause][.]

When lunchtime arrived, John ate the cheeseburger.

The dependent marker here is "when". "When lunchtime arrived" is not a complete sentence (though it can be a complete line of dialog, if it's the answer to a question). "Lunchtime arrived" is a complete sentence. It's the "when" which makes it into a dependent clause.

Remember, dependent markers tend to involve cause and effect, timing, and comparison.

Pattern 3b: Dependent Participle Clause at the Beginning

[DEPENDENT PARTICIPLE clause][,] [independent clause][.]

Another way to create a dependent clause is with a participle, a particular verb form. It's easiest to explain by example:

Sitting in his favourite chair, John ate the cheeseburger.

Given his choice, John ate the cheeseburger.

Having been given a choice, John ate the cheeseburger.

Not being a vegan, John ate the cheeseburger.

Be careful with this pattern. You need to make sure that the initial modifier is modifying the subject of the sentence, and not, for example, the subject of the previous sentence, or an understood subject of the discussion as a whole, or the speaker even though the speaker is not the grammatical subject of the sentence. The section on Dangling Modifiers in the Clarity of Reference chapter goes into more detail on this common pitfall.

Pattern 3c: Dependent Clause with Dependent Marker at the End

[INDEPENDENT CLAUSE]{,} [dependent marker] [dependent clause]

John ate the cheeseburger because he felt hungry.

The comma is optional:

John ate the cheeseburger, because he felt hungry.

Using the comma divides the sentence more obviously into a fact and its explanation.

Not all dependent markers are as comma-compatible as "because". Consider this sentence:

***~~John ate the cheeseburger, when lunchtime arrived.~~

I don't have a definite rule here, but it seems to me that the dependent markers that indicate time don't go well with the comma:

as and *since* (if they're used to indicate time, rather than logical consequence), *when, whenever, after, before, until, while.* The dependent markers that indicate logical connection, like *as* and *since* used in their logical sense, *although, as if, because, even if, even though, if, in order to, though, unless, whatever,* or *whether,* can use the comma or not—author's choice.

By the way, some of these words can be used in sentences like:

> John asked Henrietta whether she would like a cheeseburger.

In those cases, there is no comma. You don't pause before saying what John asked Henrietta.

If in doubt, leave the comma out (for this pattern).

Pattern 3d: Dependent Participle Clause at the End

[INDEPENDENT CLAUSE]{,} [dependent participle clause][.]

> John ate the cheeseburger sitting in his favourite chair.

Again, the comma is optional:

> John ate the cheeseburger, sitting in his favourite chair.

In this specific example, the comma removes any ambiguity about whether it was John or the cheeseburger sitting in the chair.

These aren't the only possible sentence patterns, of course. There are compound-complex sentences, for example, which combine several of the above patterns. Those will do to be going on with, though, and anything larger you build out of these patterns should follow the same rules.

Writing the Long Sentence

IF ALL OF YOUR SENTENCES are short, your prose becomes choppy and tedious. A fellow reviewer of mine often complained about the "declarative sentence parade," where nearly every sentence is a short, simple sentence that declares "X did Y" or "A was B". This ceases to be interesting quite quickly, and if you always write this way, your readers may be bored without knowing exactly why. You will also have difficulty conveying more complex ideas. Sometimes, a long sentence is necessary.

As a teenager, I was an arrogant little snot (but I repeat myself). I handed in to my English teacher an essay in which I had written a sentence that went on for an entire page, basically to show that I could do it. It was a grammatically valid sentence, but my teacher asked me not to do that again, and I didn't. Nor should you, unless you are parodying an old-fashioned and self-consciously erudite style of writing, and probably not even then.

You will sometimes see a particularly long sentence described as "run-on". This isn't technically correct unless it should be two sentences grammatically, and is missing punctuation at the point where the two sentences join. If it has a comma at the join point, that's a comma splice, which is incorrect, but you can join two sentences with a semicolon, as I've discussed above. This is a valid thing to do if the two sentences are closely linked in their meaning or subject, though it's best not to do it too often.

I still write a long sentence occasionally, but I'm more aware now of making long sentences easy to follow. One of the ways I do this is to think about the position of the most important piece of information, which usually involves the main verb.

Here's my final version of a sentence in a review I wrote:

It's deeply refreshing just seeing anyone writing today who has an understanding of how much social attitudes have changed in the past few centuries, or even decades (and that today's can be a bit ridiculous).

Compare this for clarity to my first draft:

Just seeing anyone writing today who has an understanding of how much social attitudes have changed in the past few centuries, or even decades (and that today's can be a bit ridiculous) is deeply refreshing.

The revision relocates the long noun phrase beginning "anyone" so that it doesn't split up the main clause. That way, the reader doesn't have to hold the start of the main clause in their head while they make their way through the noun phrase to get to the verb.

Learning to think about your sentences like this and taking the time to revise them for clarity is a useful skill, and your readers will be happier if you practice it. I'll talk more about clarity in the Clarity of Reference chapter.

I hope I've helped you understand that punctuation isn't arbitrary. You can't just put a comma anywhere you like, or leave them out if you don't feel like typing them. There are places where they're essential, or where leaving them out changes the meaning.

Chapter 7: Capitalization, Hyphenation and Punctuation

I'm grouping capitalization, hyphenation and punctuation (other than commas) together for convenience. There are a lot of subtle and not-so-subtle errors you can make with these.

Capitalization

Capitals are used for several different reasons. These include:

- Beginning a sentence

- The pronoun "I"

- Names and titles of people

- Place names

- Names of brands or trademarked objects

- Objects of special importance

- Abbreviations

They are *not* used for generic names of things in modern English. (Though they were used that way in older English, and are used that way in modern German.)

Let's go through these. If you don't use capitals to begin your sentences, or for people's names, or for "I", in the manuscripts you're submitting or the books you're self-publishing, then you have more issues than I can probably help you with, or are doing something experimental that I probably can't talk you out of. I can understand why, if you're in a casual environment like social media and typing fast or on a mobile device, you might skip these capitals, though ideally it's best to appear professional at all times (people do judge your writing by your social media communication, if you're an author). Let's move on from those straightforward cases, though, to something with more complex rules: people's titles.

Titles, Terms of Address, and Names

IF YOU'RE TALKING ABOUT "the king," "your mom," or "the colonel," you don't need capitals. However, if you're talking about "the King of England," "King Henry" or "Colonel Baird," you do—both for the name and also for the title. Basically, if there's an element (whether it's a placename, like "England," or a person's name) that has a capital, and a title's associated with it, the title gets a capital as well: Brother Eusebius, Reverend Skudder, Father Brown, Officer Friendly, Agent Gibbs, Detective Bell, Governor Grey, President Truman, Doctor Watson, Professor Challenger, Aunt Agatha, Cousin Goober. (In American usage especially, you can get away with dropping the capital if the title occurs after the name: Michael Bloomberg, mayor of New York City.)

The title also gets a capital if you're using it as a term of address, since it's standing in for a name. "Hi, Mom!" requires the capital. So does "Good morning, Colonel."

You also use the capital if you're using their title as if it was a name:

> "I'll tell Mother!"

> "I'm leaving now, Dad."

> "I inherited this from Grandma."

This usage, as applied to terms like "Dad" and "Mom" and "Auntie" especially, developed during the 20th century. You won't necessarily see it in books published prior to about the 1930s, but it is current usage.

The capital does not apply in cases like this:

> "I'll see you later, brother."

"What's happening, cousin?"

"I'm proud of you, son."

The distinction is not generational (as I thought it might be for a moment), but instead is that you wouldn't use the bare relationship word if you were speaking about these people in the third person. You'd say:

"I'll see my brother later."

Rather than:

~~"I'll see Brother later."~~

You might use the words Father, Mother, Uncle, Aunt, Grandma, Grandpa, etc. as if they were the people's names, whether you were addressing them directly or talking about them in the third person, but you don't do the same with brothers, sisters, cousins, wives, husbands, sons or daughters, any more than you would with "dude," "mate," or "buddy". ("Buddy" can, of course, be a nickname standing in for a name, in which case it has the capital.)

Also, when you do say "my dad" instead of "Dad," you're using the generic relationship term. That's why this example is correct:

"Let's ask my dad. Hey, Dad!"

In the first sentence, "my dad" is not capitalized, because it's the generic relationship term, like "my brother". In the second sentence, "Dad" is capitalized, because it's used like a name.

Regardless of your feelings about religion, if you're using *God* to refer to a specific deity (even one you don't believe in), it's a name or title, and should be capitalised. If you're talking about *a god* or *a sun god*, using the term generically, it isn't, though *the God of Poetry* or *the Sun God* (for example) get the capitals, because they're specific characters.

The use of a capital when referring to God or Christ by the pronoun *He* is falling out of use, even among Christians, but I would use it if I was portraying the speech of a devout believer or someone from earlier times.

The Bible, the Quran, the Torah and the Diamond Sutra all get capitals, but if you're using "bible" generically (*the show's story bible*) it doesn't.

Some publications will have a specific "house style" that differs from this in some detail or other. For example, some publications italicise "the *Bible*" on the grounds that it's a book title, even though that's not the traditional usage. Unless you are the editor, or write for the publication all the time, you don't have to know every nuance of the house style. Just be consistent, and follow the usual rules (which are the ones I give above), and the editor will fix it up to follow the style.

Placenames

PLACES ALSO GET CAPITALS, and the rule is similar to the rule with people's names. Refer to *the river* but *the Mississippi River*, *the ocean* but *the Pacific Ocean*, *the lake* but *Lake Placid*, *the desert* but *the Sahara Desert*. I often see writers miss out the capital on the ocean/river/lake/desert/plain/mountain/street part, and that's not correct if you're referring to a specific place by name. Likewise *Lincoln's Inn*, *St Margaret's Church*, *Cambridge University*, but *the inn*, *the church* (if you mean a building; the Church is the organisation as an abstract whole), *the university*.

The North is a place, but *north* is a direction, and doesn't get a capital. *The West Bank* is a specific place, and gets the capital, but *the west bank of the river* doesn't, because it's a generic place—many different rivers have west banks.

Now, you can make a case for capitalising, for example, "the River" if this particular river is extremely important and everyone knows which one you mean when you say "the River". That's fine. But don't deny it its capital when it's part of the name of a specific river.

Names of Things

A SIMILAR RULE APPLIES with very important items, like *the Ring* in Tolkien's *Lord of the Rings*. (Watch out for Fantasy Noun Disease, in which you capitalise every second thing and fill your sentences with strange names and titles. You'll lose most readers very quickly). Official names of things, like *the White House, the Department of the Interior* or *the Royal Canadian Mounted Police*, get capitals (though not for minor words, like "of" and "the"), but generic nouns like *department* and *police* don't.

Generic nouns in general don't get capitals: *a glass of vodka, a brougham, an oak tree.* (Don't laugh, I've seen all of those capitalised.) If you go around capitalising nouns all the time, you sound either German or 18th-century, which is fine if that's your intention, not fine if it isn't.

Generic nouns don't get capitals, but trademarks do, so *a glass of Smirnoff, a Xerox copy, an iPhone.* Use the spelling and capitalisation that's official for the brand, which means if you're not sure, look it up. (If you are sure, it's still a good idea to look it up, in case you're wrong. When I worked as an editor, my mantra was, "Always check everything, even the things you think are right." It saved me from several embarrassing mistakes.)

Languages and nationalities get capitals, even when they're not acting as nouns: *Asian cuisine, my French teacher* (but *my geography teacher*), *the Greek alphabet*. Religions, also: *a Jewish skullcap, Buddhism, he's Presbyterian*.

Specific days get capitals: Easter, Christmas, Remembrance Day, Tuesday. Seasons don't: summer, winter (unless they're in a phrase like "the Winter Palace").

In general, the rule for capitals is:

> *If it's a generic term, it doesn't get a capital. If it's the name of something specific, a title that's part of someone's name, or standing in place of a person's name, it does.*

Abbreviations

SOME COMMON ABBREVIATIONS, like *i.e.* and *e.g.*, are conventionally written in lowercase (without capitals). Incidentally, i.e. means "that is" and e.g. means "for example"; some people get them the wrong way round.

Other abbreviations, like *OK*, are conventionally written in capitals. (You can spell it *okay*, without a capital, but don't write it as ~~ok~~. That looks particularly odd when you start a sentence with it and the O is capitalised: ~~Ok~~. I see this a lot, and it looks like the speaker is an orangutan with a speech impediment.)

Be aware of abbreviations that use small letters as well as capitals, like PhD (which is short for the Latin for "Doctor of Philosophy") and pH (the measure of acidity). Make sure you get the capitals and lowercase letters in the correct place.

You'll notice that sometimes abbreviations have periods in and sometimes not. The trend is away from using periods in acronyms

(IBM, not I.B.M.—especially since it's no longer an acronym for International Business Machines, just a three-letter name). If the abbreviation has periods, it has periods after each letter—don't miss off the last one.

If you use abbreviations, check on the usual styling in a style guide such as the *Chicago Manual of Style* (CMOS), or in a dictionary. Follow the most common practice, which will be the first one listed, and be consistent, and you'll be fine. This is general advice for everything that isn't covered here specifically, by the way.

In America, abbreviations for titles, like Mr. and Dr., require a period at the end. In Britain, the rule is that if the abbreviation ends with the same letter as the full word, no full stop is necessary. If I'm writing for an American publication, I follow the American style. In either case, though, the titles begin with a capital letter if they're part of a name. As for other titles, though, if they're used generically, they don't get a capital:

He's a professor.

The doctor will see you now.

"Hey, mister!"

Some modern stylebooks are moving away from using capitals in abbreviations, which is potentially confusing. I'm thinking of a book (fiction, but written by an academic who was probably used to following a particular academic publication style) that had all abbreviations in lower case with no periods. This meant that every time he used the abbreviation for "United States" I thought for a moment he was using the pronoun "us". That wasn't the only reason I didn't finish his book—it was also quite dull—but it was definitely a factor. If you're writing fiction, rather than nonfiction within a specific style that has different rules for capitals, follow the rules as above, and look up the capitalization in a general style guide or a specific dictionary or online source.

If the publication you're writing for has an unusual style, unless they say in their submission guidelines that all submissions must follow that style, the main thing is to be consistent and follow the normal conventions, so that the copy editor has an easier job of putting your work into the house style.

Hyphenation

Another common error, which is becoming more common, is over-hyphenation. Authors have picked up the vague idea that hyphens go between adjectives and nouns sometimes, and haven't learned when that happens and when it doesn't.

Hyphens (-) do two main jobs. They join together compound nouns and compound adjectives.

Compound nouns are discussed in the Nouns chapter. Joining two nouns together with a hyphen is only one way of making them a compound (some form one word, some are written as two words with no hyphen). There aren't any rules for when to write them one way rather than another, so you need to look it up.

Compound adjectives occur when you string together a number of words (not all of which are necessarily adjectives themselves) to describe a noun:

> It was a once-in-a-lifetime opportunity.

I'll go into this in more depth in the following section.

Do not use a hyphen to join together an adjective and the noun it modifies (such as the adjective "magical" and the noun "creatures" in the following example, in case the strikethrough makes the hyphen difficult to see):

> ~~I saw several magical-creatures clustered around him.~~

There's one other place that I often see authors leaving hyphens out: the numbers twenty-one to ninety-nine inclusive. If you spell these numbers out, make sure to include the hyphens.

Don't, however, put hyphens in hundreds (in case it's not clear because of the strikethrough, there's a hyphen between "three" and "hundred" in the following incorrect sentence):

~~The vampire had lived for three-hundred years.~~

Don't hyphenate thousands, millions, or billions either.

Compound Adjectives (and other things easily confused with them)

YOU MIGHT WANT TO REVIEW the section on adjectives (words that describe or modify nouns) before continuing.

Adjectives can be single words, but they can also be phrases. Not all of the parts of an adjectival phrase have to be adjectives (just as not everything in a noun phrase has to be a noun), but the phrase as a whole acts as an adjective:

The fifteen-year-old computer was covered in dust.

Here, "fifteen-year-old" is an adjectival phrase or compound adjective. "Fifteen" and "old" are both adjectives, but "year" is a noun. The whole phrase is functioning as an adjective because it modifies the noun "computer" and tells us more about it.

Compound adjectives occur when you string together a number of words (not all of which are necessarily adjectives themselves) to describe a noun:

It was a once-in-a-lifetime opportunity.

The British rule is that you should always use the hyphens. The American rule is that you only need to use them when not using them would be ambiguous. My view is that if you use them all the time, then you don't have to think about whether not using them would make your words ambiguous.

For example, there's a difference between a *heavy-metal detector* (which detects heavy metals) and a *heavy metal detector* (which detects metals, and is heavy). There's a difference between a *stolen property report* (a report about a property, and the report has been stolen) and a *stolen-property report* (a report about some stolen property). There's a considerable difference between *six-hundred-pound dogs* (dogs that weigh six hundred pounds) and *six hundred-pound dogs* (dogs that each weigh a hundred pounds, and there are six of them). I've seen a reference to "~~seventy-two year-old arms~~" in one book where the author meant "seventy-two-year-old arms". In case it's not clear, he'd left out the hyphen between "two" and "year," leaving a phrase that read literally as referring to seventy-two arms, each of them a year old.

Compound adjective versus compound adverb

IN THE PHRASE "THE child is two years old," the words "two years old" are in fact a compound adverb, since they are modifying the verb *is*.

Compare these sentences:

> The ever-faster cycles of the machine.

> The machine cycled ever faster.

In the first sentence, "ever-faster" modifies "cycles," which is functioning as a noun. Therefore, it's an adjective, and can take the hyphen.

In the second sentence, "ever faster" modifies "cycled," which is functioning as a verb. Therefore, it's an adverb, and does not take the hyphen.

For the same reason, don't hyphenate phrases like this:

I went to see her in person.

Again, it's an adverb (that's how I went to see her) not an adjective, as it would be if I said:

We had an in-person interview.

(Compound adjective, modifying the noun "interview".)

Also, don't hyphenate compounds including "very" or other adverbs:

A very important meeting

A richly endowed foundation

(Good style advice is to avoid *very* in any case, and think of a stronger adjective in the first place: *a vital meeting*, for example. But sometimes *very* has its place.)

Note: Adding "-ly" to an adjective often transforms it into an adverb, but bear in mind that not every adverb ends in '-ly' and not every word that ends in '-ly' is an adverb. *A word is an adverb if it modifies a verb*, so "better," "best," "contrarywise," "upward," "tenfold," "leftmost," "not," "downstage" and "anew" can all function as adverbs, while, for example, "only," "likely," "earthly," "friendly" and "soldierly" are not adverbs but adjectives. It's their function, not their shape, that determines whether they are one or the other.

Compound adjective versus adjective plus noun

AMONG THE SEVERAL WAYS I've seen writers over-hyphenate, one of the more common is adding hyphens to a phrase which is an adjective plus a noun, but is similar to a frequently used compound adjective.

For example: *during the 19th century* (adjective "19th" plus noun "century") vs *a 19th-century novelist* (compound adjective "19th-century" modifying noun "novelist"); *he was twenty years old* (adjective "twenty" plus noun "years") vs *a twenty-year-old man* (compound adjective "twenty-year-old" modifying noun "man").

English being English, you can drop out the well-understood noun and talk about a *twenty-year-old*. But if you're saying "the man is twenty years old," don't use the hyphens, because then it isn't a compound adjective—it's not modifying a noun. That's a common mistake, particularly among journalists.

Do not hyphenate a phrase in which the second part is functioning as a noun, rather than as part of a compound adjective.

Compound adjective vs verb plus preposition

THIS PART DOESN'T ALWAYS involve hyphenation, but I'm leaving it here because it does involve compound adjectives.

There are a number of phrases that form one word or a hyphenated word when they are adjectives, but two when they are a verb-plus-preposition phrase, such as: *stand out, set up, sign in*. A preposition is a word that has to do with location (literal or figurative), such as *out, up, in, on, under, from*. See the Prepositions section for more about them.

> The Beatles stand out among bands of the 1960s for their popularity among their fans.

(Verb and preposition.)

> The Beatles gave a standout performance.

(Adjective.)

> The Beatles set up for their gig.

(Verb and preposition.)

> It's quite a setup you have here.

(Noun.)

> We need an hour's setup time to get it ready.

(Adjective.)

> Sign in with the app.

(Verb and preposition.)

> Please record your details on the sign-in sheet.

(Adjective.)

During the Covid emergency, I was repeatedly, though mildly, annoyed by the New Zealand government's tracer app poster, which exhorted readers:

******"~~Sign-in. Stop the virus~~."

(There's a hyphen between "sign" and "in"). In this context, "Sign in" is a verb and a preposition functioning as a phrase; it's not an adjective, and so it shouldn't get the hyphen.

Other Punctuation

I read a book once on an aspect of writing craft—not writing mechanics, which is what I'm covering here, but a particular storytelling skill. It had some good content, but it was poorly organised, and the punctuation was practically random. It read as if the author didn't know when to use specific punctuation marks, so she just shoved one in every so often and hoped for the best.

This isn't a good strategy if you want people to take your writing seriously.

In this section, I'll cover all of the common punctuation marks except for the apostrophe, capital letter, comma, and hyphen, all of which I've covered already. I'm going to do a separate chapter on punctuating dialog, so this chapter won't go into detail about how to do that.

What I will cover is: the colon; the semicolon; the dash; the parenthesis; the ellipsis; the question mark; the exclamation mark; and the period or full stop.

Colons and Semicolons

I'VE JUST DEMONSTRATED one way to use the colon and semicolon in that previous sentence.

A **colon** (:) introduces a list. A **semicolon** (;) can be used instead of a comma to separate items in a list. It's especially useful if some of the items in the list have commas in them, because then it's clear when you've started a new item:

> I saw three groups: my sisters; my brother, his wife, and their children; and my parents.

Just then, I used a colon to introduce an example (after the word "item"). That's more something you'd do in nonfiction than in fiction.

The other way to use a colon is like this: after an independent clause (one that could stand on its own as a sentence), which introduces another phrase to complete the thought. Make sure that the introductory phrase could stand on its own as a sentence, though. This is a fancy technique. Use it carefully, and only if you fully understand it.

Style guides differ on whether you should use a capital letter (that you wouldn't otherwise use) after a colon. Generally, you're safe not using the capital. Just be consistent.

As well as separating objects in lists, semicolons can be used as balance points; they can join together two independent clauses that contrast, link logically, or, together, form something that is greater than the sum of its parts. (Again, that last sentence was an example of what it described.) I used to do this all the time, but my friends kindly pointed out that it sounds pretentious, and I started trying to cut down. My advice is to do it only for deliberate effect, though I probably still do it more than is ideal.

Dashes and Parentheses

IN A MANUSCRIPT, A **dash** is indicated by two hyphens following one another, with no space between and *no space before or after*:

WORD PROCESSING PROGRAMS will often change this into an em dash, which looks like this:

FOR PURPOSES OF SUBMITTING your manuscript, either turn them all into dashes (or let your word processing program do it), or else leave them all as double hyphens. Don't mix the two up. I usually leave the double hyphens when I'm submitting to a short story market.

If you're self-publishing, convert them all to proper dashes. Make sure they're the wider em dashes (—), not the shorter en dashes (–) which are used, in typography, between two numbers to indicate a range. It looks unprofessional and unfinished to leave the double hyphens in a published book.

You can use a **single dash** to indicate that someone has interrupted themselves:

Have you seen—oh, hello, Colin.

Parentheses are sometimes called round brackets, and look like this:

()

Dashes and parentheses do the same job, which is why I'm discussing them together. They separate off a part of the sentence where you are (in effect) interrupting yourself to add some more detail—necessary or not—before getting back to your main point. And I've just demonstrated them both in one clumsy sentence.

If you're using dashes and parentheses in this way, make sure that you could remove the whole section that they surround, and the remaining sentence would still make complete grammatical sense.

The choice between dashes and parentheses is a matter of style and emphasis. You can also use parenthetical commas in the same way. Parentheses make it more obvious that you're interrupting yourself, and commas make for less of a separation between the thoughts. Dashes are in the middle. I often revise sentences by turning commas into dashes, for more separation, or parentheses into dashes, for a smoother flow.

Do not use a single parenthesis under any circumstances. If you open them, make sure you close them. Don't leave your readers hanging.

Ellipses

AN ELLIPSIS (PLURAL: ellipses) consists of three dots:

...

It is not two dots. It is not six dots. It is not however many dots you feel like typing at the time. It is three dots.

If it's at the end of the sentence, it can be followed by a period or full stop, making four dots in all, but it's also acceptable to just use the three. Pick one of these styles, and be consistent.

Different style guides differ on whether you should have a space before the ellipsis. The most common practice (and the one that's consistent with most other punctuation) is to have no space before it. There is a space after it, though.

An ellipsis, like a single dash, indicates that someone has interrupted themselves, or trailed off, leaving the thought incomplete....

The dash indicates more of an interruption, and the ellipsis more of a trailing off.

Ending a Sentence

THERE ARE THREE PUNCTUATION marks which you can use to end a sentence in English. Use one of them for any given sentence, but *only one*.

The **question mark** (?) is used to mark the end of a sentence which is a question:

But how did the bear get into the Jeffries tube?

Always use it if your sentence is a question, unless you're noting that the speaker didn't inflect it as a question. It takes precedence over the exclamation mark. If your sentence is both a question and an exclamation, use the question mark (not the exclamation mark, and certainly not both, though this is an increasingly common practice).

Questions typically involve the words *who, what, when, where, why* or *how*, but can also be phrased in other ways:

Did you see the bear?

Is this the aardvark?

Are you serious?

And he asked you if you'd come with him?

Part of what the question mark is indicating is the rising tone in a person's voice at the end of the sentence. Some people use this "high rising terminal" for sentences that are not questions—usually out of insecurity, though it can be a feature of some dialects—and you can legitimately use the question mark to show that this is what they're doing, if you indicate in the text that the speaker is one of those people.

You can also get away with not using a question mark for something phrased as a question if the speaker's tone indicates that it is not really a question (that is, it's rhetorical, or a statement in the form of a question):

This is the aardvark, isn't it.

Do not use it if your sentence is not a question:

He asked how the bear got in the Jeffries tube.

Here, the sentence reports that someone asked a question, but you are not phrasing the sentence as a question, so it does not get a question mark. It's what's known as a "narrative report of speech act," which doesn't give the exact phrasing of the speech but summarizes its content.

Do not use a question mark after the dialog tag "asked":

~~*"How did the bear get in the Jeffries tube", he asked?~~

Perhaps the one or two people I've seen doing this are thinking of this (correct) usage:

How did the bear get in the Jeffries tube, you ask? Well, I'll tell you.

Use *one* question mark, not two, not three, not however many you feel like typing at the time.

The **exclamation mark** (!) indicates that a sentence (which is not a question) is an exclamation. As a general rule, only use it in dialog. You should not be exclaiming your narrative. It makes you sound overexcited, or twelve years old, or both. (Or as if you're ranting, such as in the case of one prominent science fiction author who sprinkles exclamation marks through his narrative and is also well known for ranting on social media.)

Use only *one* exclamation mark, not two, not three, not however many you feel like typing at the time.

Do not use an exclamation mark if you are using a question mark.

The **period or full stop** (.) ends a sentence which is not a question or an exclamation.

Use only one full stop. Three full stops make an ellipsis (see above). If you put an ellipsis at the end of the sentence, you can add a full stop for a total of four dots.

After the final punctuation of a sentence (question mark, exclamation mark or full stop/period), type one space before starting the next sentence. If you learned to type on a typewriter, you may have been taught to use two spaces, but for typesetting, one space has been the industry standard since the mid-20th century, and all the major style guides now agree: one space is correct.

A poorly punctuated manuscript or book feels choppy and awkward, and the reader will be distracted from the story by trying to figure out what the author means. In a well-punctuated text, the punctuation disappears into the background, as it should. Most readers won't know why it feels smooth and professionally written, but it will.

Chapter 8: Dialog Conventions

Dialog*—characters talking—is one of the key parts of almost any story you will write. There are specific conventions around writing dialog, and if you demonstrate that you don't know them, it will be difficult for readers who do know them to take you seriously (or concentrate on the story). The conventions are there to signal which parts are narrative and which parts are people talking, and for smooth reading, it's important to follow the conventions consistently.

*I'll use the American spelling for "dialog," because it's shorter.

Dialog Tags

Let's start out by defining a term. I'll be talking a lot about **dialog tags** or "tagging" dialog. You can think of this as like a luggage tag: it tells you who the dialog belongs to. The basic dialog tag is "he said" or "she said" or "said Ashley" (if your character is called Ashley).

If you don't put in enough dialog tags, your readers will lose their way, especially if your characters sound similar to one another and there's nothing in what they say that indicates who is speaking—which might be a stylistic fault that you should work on, if it occurs all the time. If your reader has to go back and count on their fingers from the last dialog tag to work out who said what, you've lost their immersion in the story.

If you put in too many dialog tags, on the other hand, it slows down the exchange, and your readers may feel that you're treating them like idiots. If there are only two people in the scene, you don't need to tag very often to keep it clear who said what. We know they're alternating.

Your beta readers should tell you if you're tagging too often or too seldom.

Beats

"Beats" are an alternative to dialog tags. A beat is not a reference to who is speaking, but an action that the character takes during dialog:

> "So tell me about your date." John took a long slurp on his milkshake.
>
> "I turned up late, and that was the best thing about the evening."

The convention is that if the beat occurs in the same paragraph as the line of dialog, then both the dialog and the action belong to the same character. As the example above stands, we assume that John is speaking the first line and someone else is speaking the second line. If we moved the beat from after the first line of dialog to before the second, we would assume that John was the second speaker.

A beat, unlike a tag, is punctuated as a separate sentence when it occurs before or after the dialog:

> "So tell me about your date." He took a long slurp on his milkshake.
>
> Joe swallowed his bite of hamburger. "I turned up late, and that was the best thing about the evening."

But if a beat interrupts a line of dialog, it's punctuated as one continuous sentence, usually with dashes to set off the beat:

"I turned up late"—he took a long slurp on his milkshake—"and that was the best thing about the evening."

If you insert a beat in the middle of the dialog, you need to close the quotation marks for the beat, and open them up again after it, as in the example above. Don't do this:

> **"~~The wind's coming from that direction (he pointed to the west), pushing the clouds away in that direction (he pointed to the east), listen!"~~

Instead:

> "The wind's coming from that direction"—he pointed to the west—"pushing the clouds away in that direction"—he pointed to the east. "Listen!"

In the example given, the minor sentence "Listen!" was also incorrectly joined to the previous sentence with a comma splice. I left it in because it provided a piece of dialog after the end of the second beat.

Beats have a few functions. They prevent the scene from feeling like disembodied heads talking in a white room; they can provide characterisation and setting detail; they can convey emotion; and they provide a touch of variety, a relief from "he said," "she said".

Varying Tags

While I'm talking about varying tags, there are different schools of thought on how much to vary them. Many writing teachers are firm that you should only ever use "said," because this enables the dialog tags to disappear from the reader's awareness. They become almost subliminal cues that don't draw attention to themselves. Even "asked" and "replied" are a step too far for some experts. The reader can tell from the punctuation that a question was asked and replied to, they say. You don't need to make it explicit.

A much smaller group of teachers recommend what are sometimes called "said bookisms," fancier synonyms for "said" like "ranted," "uttered," "declared," or "asseverated". These create a specific style, old-fashioned, formal, and ornate. If that's the style you're going for, and you have the writing chops to pull it off (very few people do, and of those who don't, many of them don't know that they don't), then by all means use them. If you're attempting "invisible" style, though—and my advice is that you learn to write invisibly first—don't go near them.

I hold a middle view. I think it's fine to use words like "whispered" or "muttered" in place of "said" from time to time. I'll occasionally throw in an "asked" or "replied". But none of my characters "elucidate" unless I'm imitating a particular style.

I will admit that I'm very fond of Tom Swifties, which are punning phrases like this:

> "I shouldn't have sent the second telegram," Tom Swift said remorsefully.

"You gave me CPR?" said Tom, repulsed.

"I try new things for a living!" Tom protested.

They are named for the Tom Swift series of pulp adventure stories, in which Tom often said something adjectivally or with some other word than "said". Tom Swifties are a cheerful mockery of this style, and while they're a lot of fun, I don't recommend using them (or anything similar to them) in serious fiction writing.

Tag Order

There are two parts to a tag: the "said" (or, possibly, equivalent), and the identifier, the name or pronoun or other reference to who is speaking. Within limits, you can vary which comes first.

"Why did it have to be snakes?" he said.

"Why did it have to be snakes?" said Indiana Jones.

"Why did it have to be snakes?" Indiana Jones said.

"Why did it have to be snakes?" said the archaeologist.

"Why did it have to be snakes?" the archaeologist said.

You'll notice one construction missing from that list:

"Why did it have to be snakes?" said he.

"Said he" is old-fashioned and draws attention to itself, placing the emphasis on the "he". Use it sparingly, and only for deliberate effect, if you use it at all. Oddly enough, in the other examples, placing the identifier first puts a subtle emphasis on the identifier (in my opinion; you may have a different reaction). Of all of these examples, the first two are the most neutral and invisible, which is usually what you want.

If you're using a pronoun, make sure it's clear what the reference is. This is a general rule, not just for dialog. "He" refers to the last male character specified, "she" to the last female character specified, and especially if you've changed your sentence round during editing, the reference can become ambiguous.

Be especially careful if you have only two characters, of the same gender, in conversation. "He said" or "she said" then don't help the reader figure out who's speaking. You need to use names or descriptions instead.

Tagging Before, During and After

YOU CAN TAG IN THREE different places: before the dialog, during the dialog or after the dialog.

Tagging before lets the reader know who's about to speak, which can be important to how they read it, but it also draws extra attention to the identity of the speaker, and that may or may not be where you want to put the emphasis.

The colonel said, "Load of nonsense. No such thing."

Tagging during the dialog allows you to break at a significant moment in order to emphasise something or make it more dramatic.

"Snakes," said Indiana Jones. "Why did it have to be snakes?"

Make sure your break comes at a natural place, between sentences or at some other grammatical boundary, or it will sound awkward and risk confusing the reader. Bad example:

*"You crack me so consistently," said Fat Tony, "up".

There, you'd be better served by using an ellipsis to indicate the pause, especially as the grammar is odd to begin with.

Tagging after the dialog is most neutral and invisible:

"Get that aardvark out of here!" said Aunt Nora.

Punctuating Dialog

I've been showing you examples of punctuating dialog, without drawing attention to it. Now it's time to think about the conventions. I've seen authors get every one of these wrong at one time or another.

A line of dialog and its tag form a single sentence. This sentence follows all the rules of normal sentences—begins with a capital letter, ends with either a question mark, exclamation mark, or period—but with a few twists.

Most obviously, there are quotation marks around the part that the character said. Be careful with these. Not closing them is a very common error, not opening them a less common one (but I have seen it). That usually happens because you're typing too fast.

Another problem of typing too fast is that you can easily put the space and the quotation mark round the wrong way, and end up with something like this:

~~**Marcus said" I'll be out soon."~~

The American convention is to use double quotation marks, with any quote-within-a-quote getting single quotation marks, while the British convention is the other way around. Even though I live in New Zealand, which is a British Commonwealth country, I use the American convention for quotation marks. (I blame excessive exposure to American books at a formative age.) Make sure you use the two types of quotation marks in alternation. Don't put single within single or double within double.

While I'm talking about quotation marks: some people use what are known as "scare quotes," which go like this:

He was "as usual" too engrossed.

This is, to say the least, nonstandard punctuation, and makes you look amateurish. If you need to emphasise a phrase, use *italics*. Only use quotation marks for quotations, that is, for things people say. (My use of quotation marks around "scare quotes" above is to show that this is what people call these things; I'm implicitly quoting.)

The points of transition, when you come in and out of the quotation, are important, and marked by particular punctuation. Let's look at that.

Tag Before Dialog

Doug said, "Ease it gently into the cradle. Gently!"

A TAG BEFORE THE DIALOG typically ends with a comma. You can get away with leaving the comma out, but the effect is to increase the pace of the sentence. I usually put the comma in, so that I can leave it out if I want the pace to seem brisker.

The dialog then starts with a quotation mark and a capital letter (to mark the start of a sentence). At the end of the dialog, after the sentence-closing punctuation, we get a closing quotation mark. If there are sentence boundaries inside the dialog, they are marked as usual.

Tag During Dialog

"Gently," said Doug, "we don't want to crack it."

A TAG IN THE MIDDLE of the dialog is part of a whole sentence. You need a comma before the first closing quotation mark, and another after the tag. Those aren't optional.

Because the start of the second part here (the word "we") comes in the middle of a sentence—it's not starting either the whole sentence or a sentence in the dialog—*it doesn't get capitalised.*

The closing punctuation (here, a period) goes inside the quotation marks. This is the rule whenever a quotation mark ends a complete sentence.

Tag After Dialog

"We don't want to crack it," he said.

A TAG AT THE END OF the dialog needs a comma before the closing quotation mark, in place of the period that would usually finish this sentence (but see below if it's a question or exclamation).

The sentence isn't over until the tag is finished. Do not capitalise "he" in a sentence like this, as if the tag was its own sentence. It isn't, even though the dialog is a complete sentence grammatically. Also, don't end the dialog with a period if there's a tag after it. The dialog and the tag are one sentence for purposes of punctuation.

~~**"We don't want to crack it." He said.~~

However, if you use a beat, it's usually a complete sentence by itself:

"We don't want to crack it." He frowned at me.

Not:

~~**"We don't want to crack it," he frowned at me.~~

You can also put a tag and a beat together, in which case the tag rules apply:

"We don't want to crack it," he said, frowning at me.

What if the end of the dialog has a question mark or exclamation mark, though? In the examples above where a tag follows the sentence, we've turned the period that would usually be there into a comma. We don't do that with a question mark or exclamation mark—they remain themselves. There's no comma, but otherwise the punctuation of the sentence is the same:

"Do you want to crack it?" he said.

"Don't crack it!" he said.

Note, in particular, that *"he" is not capitalised.* Again, the tag is not a sentence by itself.

Be aware that, as of 2022, Apple's "autocorrect" gets this wrong; it will change the tags in the sentences above (after a quoted sentence ending in a question mark or exclamation mark) to start with capital letters. You should find the setting and disable it, if you use an Apple device.

Speech Continuing Across Paragraphs

THERE'S ANOTHER DIALOG punctuation convention that is very well known, but I've seen at least two authors get it wrong in different ways, so I'll mention it. If the same speaker continues in the next paragraph (without any tag or beat between), you leave off the closing quotation mark in the previous paragraph, like this:

"I never knew for sure how it happened, but I have a few guesses.

"Firstly, the chameleon was somewhere in that room."

The first way I've seen this done wrong is putting in the closing quotation mark after the first paragraph, which, by convention, indicates a change of speaker. In the story I was reading, the speaker hadn't changed. It was especially confusing because that author didn't make much use of tags or beats, so it was hard to tell when the speaker did switch.

The second way I've seen it done wrong is not closing the quotation if you insert a beat or tag between the paragraphs. You need the closing quotation mark to separate the dialog from the beat or tag in this case.

Some authors frequently (accidentally) leave out quotation marks at the beginning or end of dialog. If you know this is you, take extra time and care to check before publishing.

Mental Dialog

For representing characters' thoughts, the convention is to show the thoughts in italics (with no quotation marks).

I really admire Henrietta, he thought.

If you're adding the tag "he thought," the italics are optional, but if you're representing a lot of the character's specific thoughts amongst other narration, using the italics makes it clear which are the thoughts and which are not.

Let's take a moment to discuss the conventions for telepathic speech. Some writers have made up their own, because telepathy only exists in science fiction and fantasy, so there aren't widespread conventions in normal prose. Some, for example, use a tilde (~) or some other punctuation at the front of the sentence. But usually, italics and context are enough to convey that the characters are speaking telepathically.

As a general principle, **if an existing convention and context are enough to make clear what's going on, don't invent a new convention.** Examples I've seen which I do not recommend are using the words *thee* and *hast* (in many cases, incorrectly) to indicate that characters are speaking medieval Welsh, or using italics plus single rather than double quotes to indicate character thoughts—the difference in quotation style being an excessively subtle indicator which few people would catch.

Using unfamiliar or non-standard markers like this makes people notice the convention, and you want them to forget about the mechanics of the written words and pay attention to what you're writing about. This is also why you should observe conventions in the first place.

Chapter 9: Clarity of Reference

Another category of errors I sometimes see are the ones I'm grouping under "clarity of reference". The common factor between them is that they make sentences confusing, because the words don't straightforwardly convey to the reader what the author intended. The reader has to put in extra mental effort to untangle what the author means. This is mental effort that the author should put in once to write a clear sentence, rather than forcing their (possibly) many readers to put the effort in each time.

In my day job, I often design software solutions. My philosophy there is that the developer should deal with complexity once, rather than the users having to deal with it every day. It's similar with writing.

A sentence that leads the reader to an initially wrong conclusion about its grammar and meaning, and requires them to go back and parse it again, is called a "garden-path sentence" because it leads you up the garden path. A commonly given example is:

> The complex houses married and single soldiers and their families.

The reader starts out by assuming that in "The complex houses," "complex" (adjective) modifies "houses" (noun); these are houses that are complex. You might then start to wonder why these complex houses married (verb), and then the sentence falls apart completely after "and", or at best after "single," which can be a verb as well as a noun, though it needs an "out" ("single out") to make sense.

If you go back to the beginning knowing that that interpretation is wrong, and carefully read it again, it's actually referring to a housing complex (noun), which houses (verb) married and single (adjectival phrase) soldiers and their families (noun phrase).

I don't know whether that example was originally a naturally occurring one or whether someone constructed it as a demonstration, but the examples I quote below are all from actual books I have read.

Dangling Modifiers

The most obvious, and probably most frequent, errors of reference are dangling modifiers. Modifiers are phrases which give more context to the rest of the sentence. They can come at the start or the end of the sentence. They need to be set off with commas:

Henrietta burst through the aardvark door, making me wonder what had happened.

Seizing my opportunity, I pocketed the jade bracelet.

The modifiers here are "making me wonder what had happened" in the first sentence, and "seizing my opportunity" in the second.

Modifiers carry a risk. The author Jim Butcher's Wikipedia entry used to have a sentence that started out this way:

~~***While sick with strep throat as a child, Butcher's sisters introduced him to *The Lord of the Rings*.~~

Taking advantage of Wikipedia's policy of allowing anyone to edit, I corrected this. (That last sentence also has a modifier. Did you notice?)

Can you see what's wrong with the original version of the sentence? Think through its literal meaning.

The person who originally typed that sentence presumably had a thought process that, if it had been more explicit, would have run something like this: *Jim Butcher is the subject of this article, so any sentence in it is implicitly about him.* However, what the sentence literally said was that his sisters were ill with strep throat when they introduced him to *The Lord of the Rings*. Here's my correction:

> While he was sick with strep throat as a child, Butcher's sisters...

You'll sometimes see this kind of structure discussed under the heading of **dangling participles** or **misrelated participles**. Strictly speaking, since there is no "-ing" or "-ed" form in the phrase "while sick with strep throat as a child," it isn't a participle, so I'm using the term "modifier" as a more general description.

Here are several dangling modifiers, all from the same book (slightly altered to disguise their origin—though I read a pre-publication version, so hopefully someone found and fixed them):

> ~~***Pressed against the wall, a sick dread filled him.~~
>
> ~~***After cycling open, the air smelled old.~~
>
> ~~***Plunging through an arch, the curvature of the planet was revealed.~~
>
> ~~***Pushing a hand into the interface, the grid welcomed her.~~

In all these cases, there's an implied subject that's different from the grammatical subject of the sentence. In the first case, "he" is the implied subject, and is doing the action described by the modifier ("pressing against the wall"), but the grammatical subject of the sentence is "a sick dread". In the second, the implied subject comes from a previous sentence which mentioned an airlock, which is what is cycling open, but the grammatical subject is "the air".

There's an easy fix for these, and it's to mention the intended subject explicitly. Like this:

As he pressed against the wall, a sick dread filled him.

After the airlock cycled open, the air smelled old.

As the ship plunged through an arch, the curvature of the planet was revealed.

She pushed a hand into the interface, and the grid welcomed her.

From another book:

***A professional dancer, I had first set eyes on her...

Here it's "her" (the object of the sentence), not "I" (the subject of the sentence) who is the professional dancer.

From a book on writing:

***To keep selling stories, a reader needs to identify you as the person who can hit all their buttons on a consistent basis.

Again, the reader (the subject of the sentence) is not the one selling stories here. Try:

If you want to keep selling stories, a reader needs to identify you...

The words "having" and "being" are commonly used in modifiers, and frequently end up dangling. Some examples from another book:

~~***Having won nothing, the pile of coins in my lap was almost gone.~~

~~***Being the same height, my eyes were level with hers.~~

~~***Being such a slight movement, my eyes might have missed it altogether.~~

I think we can safely assume that the author didn't intend the character to say that the pile of coins in her lap had won nothing, that her eyes were the same height as her friend (which would make them very tall eyes), or that her eyes were a slight movement. Suggestions for correction:

I had won nothing, and the pile of coins in my lap was almost gone.

We were the same height, so my eyes were level with hers.

It was such a slight movement, my eyes might have missed it altogether.

This example is an approach to the dangling modifier I'd never seen before:

~~Continuously making what the sponsors had requested, despite never coming to collect...~~

It was the sponsors, not the people who were making things, who never came to collect.

Another variation:

~~A gray suit that matched his hair, combed back away from his face~~

The hair, not the suit, was presumably combed back, but the suit is the subject.

Dangling modifiers show fuzzy thinking and, besides leading to unintentionally ridiculous scenarios, reduce the reader's confidence in you as a writer. If you let your modifiers dangle, you'll trip over them and fall on your face.

Number Agreement and Plurals

I n English, verbs can sometimes change form depending on whether the subject is singular or plural. I suspect that most of the time when people get this wrong, it's because they originally had a different subject and didn't edit their sentence properly:

~~**The problems with the magicians is...~~

Probably what happened there is that the author was going to talk about one problem, then talked about several problems, went back and changed the noun, but didn't check the sentence over to make sure that the verb was also correct. *Always, when you edit a sentence, take the extra couple of seconds to check that you've left it in a consistent state*—that your edit hasn't introduced an error.

This one might be similar:

~~**Her mouth and eyes grew to three times its normal size.~~

Here it's not the verb that's the problem (since, like most verbs other than *to be*, *grew* can be either singular or plural). The problem is the pronoun, which should be "their," not "its". Again, it may be a problem of revision: the sentence may have started out as "Her mouth grew to three times its normal size," and then the author added the eyes and forgot to change the pronoun.

Sometimes, though, number errors arise because the author is confused about the number of the noun involved. For example:

~~**He repeated this until every last one of the new recruits were complete.~~

"Every last one" behaves as a singular noun, even though it refers to multiple people. The next one is even clearer:

> **One of his legs were bandaged with cloth.

(That was in a book published by one of the largest English-language publishers in the world, by the way, in case you think these examples all come from self-published books.) "One of his legs" is a singular noun phrase, even though it has the plural noun "legs" in it.

Some real-life examples from a couple of books I read in 2022, with identifying names changed or removed, show us another problem:

> *The only reason she didn't have to squint her eyes almost entirely shut were

> *Lisa, along with most of her neighbors, were

> *The truth of Vic's words were revealed.

In all three cases, we have a plural noun (eyes, neighbors, words) which is not the subject of the sentence, but is closer to the verb than the subject is. The verb needs to reflect the number of the subject (in these examples, "the reason," "Lisa" and "the truth"), not the number of the most recent noun.

Bear in mind that if the subject is a list of things, that counts as a plural noun, even if everything in the list is individually singular:

> Jeff and I **are** coming over now.

You'd say:

> Jeff is coming over now.

I am coming over now.

But "Jeff and I" counts as a plural subject, so the verb is also plural.

This is a rule I learned the hard way. I'd written a letter to the editor of a prominent national magazine, about an article which suggested that reading standards were falling among young people. I didn't mention in the letter that I was 15 at the time, and was glad I hadn't when someone pointed out that "grammar and spelling is" should have been "grammar and spelling are".

There are some extra complexities around plurals when you are talking about groups of things. Partly it depends on whether you are mainly talking about the group or mainly talking about the individuals, and there is a wrinkle where British and American usage differs. In British English, it's correct to say "the band are on their way" (speaking as if you're talking about the individual members of the band, even though you've referred to them collectively); American English would prefer "the band is on its way".

Where it becomes harder is in phrases like "a set of things". Should the verb be plural (*a set of things are*) or singular (*a set of things is*)? It depends whether you are mainly talking about the things or the set.

Unusual Plurals

MOST PLURALS IN ENGLISH are formed by adding "s" to the base noun, and this usually applies to words that were originally from other languages, too, since if it didn't English would be even more confusing than it is. There's a counterexample in my own country, New Zealand, where there's a widespread convention that words from the indigenous language, Maori, don't take the "s" plural when used in English, since they don't change form in the plural in Maori. The fuller context is that Maori distinguishes singular from plural using different forms of the definite article (*te* for singular and *nga* for plural), a strategy English hasn't had available for about a thousand years now, since we now only use one form of the definite article, *the*. So this isn't the solution I would have suggested myself—my view is that if a word is in an English sentence it should follow English grammar, just as it would follow Maori grammar in a Maori sentence—but the decision wasn't up to me, and since that is the general usage I try to follow it. In most cases, though, if you have imported a word into English and are using it as an English word, it follows English rules for plurals.

Non-standard English plurals

There are a few English plurals that retain their old forms ending in -en (*children, brethren,* and *oxen*). There are also some plurals that form by changing the vowel instead of the ending, such as *man/men, woman/women, foot/feet, goose/geese, mouse/mice, louse/lice, tooth/teeth*. In British but not American English, the plural of *penny* is *pence*; American English uses *pennies*. There's also *die* and *dice*, though a single die (in the sense of a geometric solid rolled as a randomizer) is sometimes referred to as "a dice". These non-standard plurals are known as "apophonic" or "mutated" plurals.

In addition, there's a rule that if the singular noun ends in -f or -fe, usually (but not always) the f becomes a v in the plural: *knife/knives, life/lives, loaf/loaves, scarf/scarves, wife/wives, wolf/wolves, calf/calves, thief/thieves, leaf/leaves* (though if you're talking about several electric cars made by Nissan, these are usually referred to as "Leafs" rather than "Leaves," presumably because it's a brand name). *Hoof* can be pluralized as either *hoofs* or *hooves*; both are considered correct. But it's *roof/roofs, proof/proofs, chef/chefs, chief/chiefs, gulf/gulfs*, and most or all of the ones that end in a double f keep the f in the plural: *riff/riffs, cliff/cliffs, muff/muffs, toff/toffs*.

Relevant to fantasy fiction: Tolkien consciously decided to use *dwarf/dwarves* and *dwarven, dwarvish*, the same pattern as *elf/elves*, and that's become standard in a fantasy context, but *dwarfs* is the official plural outside that context—or even sometimes within it; the title of the Disney film from 1937 is *Snow White and the Seven Dwarfs*, though of course that predates Tolkien's widespread influence, since *The Hobbit* came out in the same year. Many people pronounce the film's name with "Dwarves" instead of "Dwarfs" now, and according to Google Ngram Viewer (of which more later), the spelling "dwarfs" and the spelling "dwarves" were about equally popular by 2020, though "dwarfs" was very much the dominant spelling prior to that. "Dwarves" started to rise in about 1965, having almost never been used previously, when the book version of *The Lord of the Rings* started to gain serious commercial traction, and the usage went up sharply starting in the early 2000s, when the Lord of the Rings movies came out.

So in fiction set in our world prior to 2020, unless you're talking about Tolkien's dwarves or other fantasy dwarves influenced by them (such as those in Dungeons & Dragons), it's safest to use the spelling "dwarfs".

All this mess goes back to Old English, and even if you're a scholar of Old English and can remember all the complicated history, it's still easier just to remember which ones get the "v" and which don't—or let your spell checker remind you.

Borrowed from other languages

Then there are some Latin, Greek, and Hebrew plurals that sometimes or always keep their Latin, Greek, and Hebrew forms.

The two I see messed up most often are *antenna* and *millennium*. I've just given you the singular forms. The plurals are *antennae* and *millennia.* (You can use *antennas* if you are talking about radio, but not usually if you're talking about insects.) I often see authors make mistakes like:

> ***~~A couple of millennium ago~~

Or:

> ***~~So it had been for a millennia.~~

Other pairs:

- One seraph or cherub, two seraphim or cherubim (anything religious with an "-im" ending is likely to be plural, and Hebrew). Seraphs and cherubs are also acceptable.

- One incubus or succubus, two incubi or succubi, though if you call them incubuses and succubuses nobody will blink.

- One hypothesis, two hypotheses. For that matter, one thesis, two (or, if you're Martin Luther, 95) theses.

Make sure, if you use these words or others like them, that you know which form is singular and which is plural.

Noun phrases with unexpected plural forms

The plural of *son-in-law* is *sons-in-law*, not "~~son-in-laws~~". The sons are plural, the law is singular. This is because son-in-law is a noun (son) with a subsequent adjective (in-law); other examples of the pattern are *governors general, courts martial, passersby, runners-up, chiefs of staff, coats of arms, poets laureate, heirs apparent, professors emeritus.* English usually puts its adjectives before its nouns, but in some old-fashioned constructions influenced by Norman French or Latin, mostly to do with the law and government or used poetically, the adjective goes after the noun. In these cases, it's the noun that gets made plural, even if the adjective is a phrase that also involves a noun (as in *chiefs of staff* or *coats of arms*).

Plural the same as singular

There are a few English plurals that are the same as the singular form.

Craft is the plural of *craft* if you are talking about vehicles (aircraft, water craft, spacecraft...). *Crafts* means activities like macrame or decoupage.

Fish is the plural of *fish*, just as *sheep* is the plural of *sheep* and *deer* is the plural of *deer*. On the same pattern, *buffalo* can be the plural of *buffalo* and *bison* is the plural of *bison*. *Horse* was also the usual plural of *horse* up to the 17th century (though *horses* started being used as early as the 13th century), but now we always say *horses* except in phrases like *a hundred horse*, meaning a cavalry unit of that size. *Fishes* means more than one kind of fish: "The native fishes of the region." In other contexts, it's: one fish, two fish, red fish, blue fish. There is no English word ~~sheeps~~ or ~~deers~~, even if you're talking about different kinds of those animals.

Types of fish are also the same in singular and plural: cod, trout, salmon, carp.

Other mismatching plurals

People is the plural of *person*, except in formal administrative or legal contexts, where the plural of *person* is *persons*; this is mainly because the legal usage includes "legal persons" like corporations, which are not people. There's also a word *peoples* that, like *fishes*, means more than one type of people: "The peoples of Stone Age Europe."

Cattle is plural, but there's no generally agreed-upon singular—oddly, given that English-speaking people have always had cattle around, but there it is. Depending where you live, it may be *cow* (though technically that's a female, it is sometimes used to refer to a male), *cattlebeast* or *head of cattle*.

Generalizations

When you're making a generalization about a group that has a collective name, there are a couple of ways you can do it:

> Lions are an endangered species.

> The lion is an endangered species.

Both of these sentences mean essentially the same thing. The second one is more formal and old-fashioned, and, these days, may come across as pretentious.

People a century ago sometimes had the habit of generalizing about whole populations using this kind of construction: "The Jew does this," "The Negro does that," "The Chinaman does this other thing." I shouldn't need to tell you that a character who stereotypes people in this way is going to come off as a villain in contemporary fiction, even if it was acceptable for heroes like John Buchan's Richard Hannay in the early 20th century.

Neither... Nor... versus Both... And

IF YOU'RE TALKING ABOUT two things or people and neither one of them has a particular quality or has done a thing, the construction goes like this:

> Neither Bill nor his friend has arrived.

Notice that the verb is singular, even though you're talking about two people. Presumably the logic is that Bill has not arrived, and his friend, acting independently, has also not arrived.

On the other hand:

Both Bill and his friend have arrived.

The verb is plural if they are both doing the thing. Bill and his friend have both arrived.

Both and Each

Speaking of "both," based on the number of examples I see it's apparently easy to confuse *both* with *each*. *Both* means that two things are sharing; *each* means that they are not.

For example:

> ****They were both wearing a suit of armour.**

I'm prepared to bet that they were each wearing a suit of armour; there were two people and two suits of armour, not one suit of armour worn by two people, which is what that sentence says.

> ****It had a rubber seal on both ends.**

Again, only one seal on both ends is unlikely. It probably had a rubber seal on each end, totalling two seals. A couple more real examples:

> ****He pulled a chair out for both of them.**

> ****She handed us both a spoon.**

Also, "two candelabra on both sides of the entrance" is a total of two, but "two candelabra on each side of the entrance" is a total of four.

Both means they're sharing, each means they're not.

Word Order

The order of the words in your sentences can change the meaning. Compare these phrases:

In a way that she could only dream of

In a way that only she could dream of

"Only" can be either an adjective or an adverb. In the first version of the sentence, it's an adverb modifying the verb "dream". In the second version, it's an adjective modifying "she".

The first sentence means that the way was something that wasn't within the bounds of practicality, that she was only able to dream about it. The second means that, unlike everyone else, she could dream of this way.

When revising, review your word order to make sure your sentences say what you intend them to. Also, that they make sense, unlike this one:

~~...this time two hitting the thugs Sarah faced each.~~

What the author meant was "this time, two each hitting the thugs Sarah faced." The "two" referred to projectiles which had been mentioned earlier.

Between

A trend I've noticed lately is to use "between" with only one object instead of two, whereas *between* inherently refers to two things, with something happening or existing inside the space which they define.

Take this example from a website:

> **~~**Certain olive trees were still alive between an ocean of death.~~**

A better preposition to use in this case would have been "amid". I've also seen it the other way round, where "amid" should be "between":

> ~~back onto the street amid two carriages.~~

Another example:

> ~~She slipped between the crooked gap in the doorway.~~

A better choice there would have been "through".

> ~~Their fingertips stretched between the distance.~~

Here, the better choice is "across".

Sometimes, the "between" is just because the sentence is incomplete:

> ~~He stood between the danger.~~

That would have been fine if the other object had been made explicit:

He stood between his friend and the danger.

This one is similar:

The two men were between my path to the door.

That author has omitted "me and" from the sentence as clearly implied:

The two men were between me and my path to the door.

It could be part of a wider phenomenon of omitting understood objects/phrases: "the archway connecting the library" [to the room she was in]. "Getting as much information" [as possible]. Or it might be the beginning of a shift in the usage of "between". Another example:

Far be it from me to stand between true love.

The clear meaning is "in the way of," but the author should say that.

You can legitimately use "between" if the object is plural:

He slipped between the sheets.

Here's one where it would have been fine if the noun "brow" was plural ("brows"), as it ought to have been:

A furrow appeared between Sarah's brow.

This one is borderline:

She pinched the lenses between a fold in her shirt.

We know what the author meant, even though there's technically only one object; the fold in the shirt is on either side of the lenses and acting as if it's plural. Still better to rephrase as "between folds of her shirt". Similarly:

~~The metal frame was wedged between a forked branch.~~

It's clear what it means—wedged between the forks of a branch—but the author should say that.

This version, though, I think the author almost gets away with:

in between the peacock's beak.

Although the beak is grammatically singular, it consists of two physical parts. It's equivalent to "jaws" in another animal. I would still rephrase:

in the peacock's beak.

Comparatives and Superlatives

Adjectives have degrees: Tall, taller, tallest. *Taller* is the **comparative** of *tall*, and *tallest* is the **superlative**.

There are a couple of different ways of forming comparatives (other than the irregular ones, like *good, better, best; much, more, most; little, less, least; bad, worse, worst*). Some words make comparatives with "-er," and others by using the word "more" before them: *quieter* but *more thoughtful*. The rough rule of thumb is: one-syllable words get "-er," three-syllable and longer words get "more," and two-syllable words can go either way (check a dictionary if you're not sure—or even if you are; you could be wrong).

Don't combine the two and say "~~more better~~" or "~~more gentler~~".

The "-er" comparatives are matched with "-est" superlatives. The "more" comparatives are matched with "most" superlatives.

If you're comparing in the other direction, it's always done with the word "less". You say "quieter" but "less quiet".

Be careful that your sentence makes complete sense when you mix the two types of comparatives:

> ****~~He was much quieter and thoughtful than his brother.~~**

Here, the author has left out the "more" before "thoughtful".

If you're making a comparison with "than," you need to use "more" or "less" rather than the "-er" version of the comparison:

> ***~~He came across as creepier than charming.~~**

He came across as more creepy than charming.

Note the following patterns to use when comparing two things:

As much a problem **as** drunkenness

More of a problem **than** drunkenness

Don't mix them up:

***As much** a problem **than** drunkenness

***More** of a problem **as** drunkenness

Don't laugh; I've seen both of these patterns, though usually with more words between the key parts. Here's a real-life example, only altered by substituting "him" for the character name to obscure the source:

*It was as much a protection from him than anything else.

Pronouns

Pronouns (I, you, they, we, he, she, it) stand in for nouns. They aren't full nouns for some grammatical purposes (for example, apostrophes).

The big problem with pronouns is ambiguity (also a problem with "this" and "that"). You need to be careful that your pronoun refers to the person you intend it to refer to. The rule is that "he" refers to the last male who was mentioned, "she" to the last female mentioned, and "it" to the last object (or animal of undetermined gender) mentioned. Especially if you revise your sentences, this may get messed up.

I saw one early draft in which the author had mentioned a crate which the main character hid behind, and then added a paragraph about another box being dragged across the floor of a warehouse. She then wrote something like, "He watched through a hole in it..." Obviously, since he wasn't in the box that was being dragged (the most recent object that "it" could refer to), this sentence was disorienting for the reader.

The other issue you are likely to hit with clarity of reference is when you have two males or two females and use pronouns for both of them indiscriminately, especially if you're flipping back and forth between the two of them without signalling. This quickly becomes confusing for the reader.

Example:

> She used a fresh handkerchief to wipe away the small streak of blood from her shoulder.

In the context of the book in which I read this, "she" is one woman and "her" refers to a different woman. However, the plain and obvious meaning is that both refer to the same woman, and that she's wiping her own shoulder. In a case like this, use names, so it's clear who is doing what to whom.

Similarly, from a different book:

> Since they'd begun helping them earlier in the winter they had warmed to the group of adventurers.

The first "they" here is the adventurers, but "them" and the second "they" refer to the townspeople. A clearer version would be:

> Since the group of adventurers had begun helping them earlier in the winter, the townspeople had warmed to them.

From the same book as the previous example:

> Andrew paid him for delivering it. He raised his eyebrow when he noted the crest on the letter.

The "him" of the first sentence is not the "he" of the second sentence; that's Andrew (character name changed to obscure the source), causing the reader to stutter and have to go back and reread.

See also the section on Relative Pronouns in the Commas of Identity chapter.

Pronoun Pitfalls

HERE ARE A FEW MORE pitfalls with pronouns.

I/Me

PEOPLE OFTEN SAY "X and I" when "X and me" is grammatically correct, or vice versa. It works like this:

> She told John and me about it.

This is correct, because you'd say "She told me about it." In other words, you can take "John and" out of the sentence and it still reads correctly. Compare these sentences:

> ****She told John and I about it.

> She told I about it.

Both of those sentences are wrong, and for the same reason. Most modern English pronouns, unlike modern English nouns, take different forms when they're subjects than they do when they're objects. "I" is a subject; "me" is an object.

The problem is probably an overcorrection of this error:

> ***John and me went to the shops.

That's equivalent to:

> Me went to the shops.

Occasionally, another pronoun gets caught in this error:

> *a shared nightmare between he and his mother

The correct pronoun there is "him".

Now that you know the rule and how to check it, it should be easier for you to get this one right. In dialog, of course, (or the implied dialog of a first-person narrator, or a close third-person narrative that represents the character's thoughts) it's fine to represent someone making the mistake if that character would do so. In dialog, all bets are off. But you should know the correct phrasing, and use it outside dialog.

Who/Whom

I'VE ONLY SEEN A COUPLE of authors get this wrong, but I'm sure there are others: The word "whom" is sometimes (decreasingly) used in formal writing. You might well use it to indicate a pedantic, careful speaker. If you do use it, though, make sure you use it correctly. "Who" and "whom" are not simple alternatives. They're like "I" and "me," in that the first is used for the subject and the second for the object.

> Who did you ask? (Correct, informal/modern)

> Whom did you ask? (Correct, formal/old-fashioned)

> I asked him who his doctor was. (Correct, formal or informal)

> *~~I asked him whom his doctor was~~. (Incorrect)

> *~~Whom was there?~~ (Incorrect)

The incorrect examples put "whom" in the subject position. If you analyse the sentences, both the doctor and the person who was there were performing the action of the verb ("to be" in this case).

Two People

I'VE SEEN OTHER AWKWARD pronoun fumbles in sentences like this:

> **For a moment she and Will's eyes met.

Read literally, that sentence says that she (the whole of her) met Will's eyes, which is an interesting image, but probably not what the author meant. Try this:

> For a moment, her eyes met Will's.

Similar is this one:

> The bounty on mine and my father's heads

I'm not sure why people write these awkward, distorted sentences when they're so easy to fix:

> The bounty on my head and my father's

Relative Pronoun Reference Errors

HERE'S A GEM:

> William readied his dagger in his left hand, which he kept strapped to his leg.

Having his left hand strapped to his leg must have made fighting, and a lot of other tasks, very difficult. Make sure that your pronouns refer to what you think they refer to (that is, the most recently mentioned qualifying noun).

The following sentence attempts to use a relative pronoun to point to the person who owns a thing rather than the thing itself, which is the grammatical reference:

~~She put on Ellie's robe, who although twelve, had long legs~~

There should be a comma after "who," as well; "although twelve" is a parenthetical comment that needs to be set off between two matched punctuation marks.

The same author also committed this one, which reads like a dangling modifier, but also involves a relative pronoun (character names have been changed in both examples to obscure the source):

~~Anna observed Miss Smith's hair with admiration, which miraculously stayed in place~~

The hair, not the admiration, stayed in place.

Gender

ANOTHER PRONOUN PITFALL is switching between "it" and "he" for animals, etc. If your characters are dealing with an animal or monster, either choose a gender for the creature and stick with that gender, or stay with "it" throughout. Don't switch between pronouns, unless something has occurred to reveal the animal's gender, in which case stick with that gender from then on; don't go back to "it". Switching back and forth is confusing to your readers, who will think, "do the 'it' and the 'he' refer to the same thing?" It's surprisingly common, though. I read one book by an author who did it constantly, not only with animals and monsters but even with human opponents in a couple of cases.

Singular They

THESE DAYS, PEOPLE are sometimes referred to by the pronoun *they*, which avoids assigning them a gender for any of a number of reasons (their gender is unknown, ambiguous, or neither male nor female, for example). There are other non-gendered pronouns, too, all of them invented, none of which have gained much traction compared to singular *they*.

Singular *they* has been used for centuries in contexts where gender is unknown, undefined, considered irrelevant, or is not specified because that would give away too much information, or in order to include both male and female without the awkwardness of "he or she". The Oxford English Dictionary cites its oldest example from the medieval romance *William and the Werewolf*, written in 1375 (though when you look at the citation in context, the previous word "eche" is what is now referred to as a distributive expression with an implied plural sense, so it may not strictly speaking be an example of singular "they"). It was used by numerous prominent writers including Jane Austen and William Shakespeare. Opposition to the usage began among grammarians in the 18th century, who had apparently forgotten the controversy about singular *you* in the 17th century.

Yes, *you* was originally plural, the singular form being *thee*. The plural was used, like the German equivalent today, as the polite singular form for a long time, until *thee* fell out of use in the 17th century in all but a few dialects and certain religious contexts. Interestingly, various dialects are now developing ways of indicating plural *you* again, such as *y'all*, *you-uns*, *yinz*, *youse* or *you guys* in America and *youse* or *yis* in Britain, all of which are (so far) considered more or less unsuitable for formal speech and writing. Perhaps, with singular *they* becoming more common, we'll eventually see a similar evolution of terms used to indicate when *they* is used in a plural sense. *They-all? All of them?*

Meanwhile, we're in a transitional time for singular *they*, with some people now adopting it deliberately as a pronoun for themselves because it doesn't constrain them to a male or female gender. This is a new usage originating in the 21st century, to be clear; the earlier usage was for a generic person who could be male or female, a person whose gender was unknown, or a person of known gender where the speaker or writer didn't want to reveal their gender by using a gendered pronoun. Some people oppose the use of singular *they* for a specific known person on various grounds, mostly political, though sometimes framed in terms of prescriptive grammar; many of the same people will use it in informal speech for generic persons, persons of unknown gender, or where both male and female genders are intended, since that usage has become more common among native English speakers than using *he* or *he or she* in those cases. The major style guides are slowly coming round to allowing this usage in formal writing, though they vary in their guidance; even those that consider singular *they* as best avoided in the context of unknown or unspecified gender often make an exception where it's a specific person's chosen pronoun.

In writing, because plural *they* is still the more common form, it can be ambiguous or confusing to the reader unless the reference to a single person is made clear by sentence structure and context. Most readers will still assume *they* refers to more than one person unless it's clearly indicated otherwise.

While singular and plural *they* both use the plural verb forms (like singular and plural *you*), some writers use *themself* rather than *themselves* as the reflexive form. This is an old usage (14th to 16th centuries), and has been growing since the 1970s, but it is not universal. Compare the now-standard *yourself* for singular *you* and *yourselves* for plural *you*.

The other pitfall to watch for when using *they* in your writing is consistency. Just as authors who write in present tense can have a tendency to slip accidentally into past from time to time, some authors who use the pronoun *they* for a character will occasionally refer to that character as *he* or *she* by mistake. If you're using *they*, be extra vigilant about this. Likewise, of course, if you change the gender of your character at some point in the revision process; it's easy to miss a pronoun here or there and leave the reader confused.

Using (or not using) *Thee* and *Thou*

IT'S TEMPTING FOR AUTHORS setting their books in historical periods (or pseudo-historical periods, as with secondary-world fantasy) to use the pronouns *thee* and *thou* to give an olde-tymey flavour to the characters' speech. I strongly recommend against doing so unless you have a really compelling reason (such as: the characters are Quakers, who kept using *thee* longer than most English speakers because of their founder George Fox's strong opposition to plural *you*) and you also know exactly what you're doing, thanks to careful study of the language of the time, or yourself being a native speaker of one of the English dialects that still use a form of *thee*.

Even then, think twice, if not more often. And then don't do it.

Most people don't have much idea how to use these words correctly. They take different verb forms from *you*, for one thing, and since those verb forms are not in use in modern speech, most modern speakers will mess them up (or just use the verb forms for *you*, which makes it even more obvious that you don't know what you're doing).

Some people who have even less idea will mix up the verb forms and use them with the wrong pronouns.

I read one particularly bad example—published, I will emphasize, by a major publisher—where the author had inexplicably decided to use the pronoun *thee* and the verb form *hast* from early modern English to indicate when the characters were speaking early medieval Welsh—something that was completely obvious from context at all times, and didn't need the extra hint. Not only did she use *thee* incorrectly, often using it where it should have been *thou*, but she used *hast* incorrectly; it was always *hast* regardless of the grammar of the sentence or which pronoun she was using it with. I hast, thee [should be thou] hast, he hast, they hast, we hast. It was awful.

That is by far the worst example I've seen, but I've also seen other attempts to use *thee* in modern writing, and I can't think of a single one that produced a good result. Don't do it unless you're an expert, and even then, don't do it unless nothing else will produce the effect you're after. And even then, preferably don't do it.

Since I'm aware that a lot of people will ignore the advice I just gave, against my better judgement I'm going to give a brief introduction to historical English and its correct usage, so that if you do insist on writing like this you have at least some chance of getting it partially correct.

First, some terminology. Old English is the language used in England after the Anglo-Saxon conquest, which began after the end of Roman rule in Britain in around the year 410. It gradually overtook the native Celtic languages in most of England until the Norman Conquest in 1066, at which point Norman French became the language of the governing classes. Old English is a Germanic language which is not comprehensible to speakers of modern English; you have to learn it like a foreign language (I know this, because I did). Some of its vocabulary was influenced by Old Norse from the Danish invaders starting around 800.

A good deal of everyday vocabulary from Old English, and some but certainly not all of the grammar, was brought forward into Middle English, the language of Chaucer, which was spoken from about 1100 to 1500. Until the 14th century, though, there's little recorded in Middle English, since Norman French was the prestige language and most literate people used it. Middle English imported a lot of vocabulary from Norman French, particularly the vocabulary of law and government. If you sit down to read a page of Middle English as a modern speaker, you'll be able to make some sense of it, but you'll need a glossary to help you with those parts of the vocabulary which have changed.

The language of William Shakespeare, who lived 1564-1616, is neither Old English nor medieval English; it's Early Modern English, as used in the Renaissance and up to about 1650. It's sometimes used to represent medieval English, and sometimes referred to as Old English, but both of these are incorrect. This is the kind of language that, for example, Marvel Comics used, or attempted to use, to represent the "old-fashioned" speech of Thor and the other Asgardians up until recently. To a modern English reader, it's English with some unfamiliar vocabulary and a couple of grammatical differences.

Apart from some specific words, the main differences are in the use of "thee" and "thou" for second person singular, and the -eth ending (instead of the more modern -es) on verbs used in the third person. People who have little grasp of Early Modern English usage are liable to mix these up and produce something both extremely inaccurate and not especially comprehensible. Let's set out a couple of tables to make things clear.

Terminology first: the *first person* is the speaker, the *second person* is the one spoken to, and the *third person* is the one spoken about. All of these, in Early Modern English, used different pronouns depending on whether they are singular (one person) or plural (more than one person); in present-day English, we no longer distinguish between second person singular and second person plural, since we now use "you" for both. Other European languages have kept the distinction, and, as in Early Modern English, it's now more about politeness than number; you only use the singular form with someone you know intimately, and the plural form is used, regardless of whether you're speaking to one or several people, if you're being polite (or if you're speaking to several people you know well).

The other distinction of pronouns is between subject (doing the action of the verb) and object (having the action of the verb done to them). Most English pronouns, including "thee/thou," have a different form for these two grammatical roles, but "you" does not, which I assume is part of the reason that people sometimes say "thee" when they mean "thou" or vice versa.

Here's the table:

Person	Subject	Object	Possessive
First (singular)	I	me	my
First (plural)	we	us	our
Second (singular)*	thou	thee	thy
Second (plural)	you	you	your
Third (singular)	he/she/it	him/her/it	his/her/its
Third (plural)	they	them	their

*No longer used in present-day English

Now, the verb forms:

I do; I have

We do; we have

Thou dost; thou hast

You do; you have

He doth; he hath (present-day forms: he does; he has)

They do; they have

Note that **only the second and third person singular forms are different**. Don't go sticking "hast" or "hath" in at random, regardless of the grammar; they have specific correct usages.

Also, the initial "t" in words like "twas" or "twould" is short for "it"; they mean "it was" and "it would". Don't use it unless you could put the "it" at the front and have it make sense.

Having said all of this, I'll repeat: **do not attempt "period" language unless you know exactly what you're doing, know what effect it will produce, and specifically want that effect despite its drawbacks**. The author Travis Baldree quotes some good writing advice he received in an interview included in one of his books: "Use words you know, in your own voice." I heartily endorse that advice in nearly all circumstances.

Non-reflexive Myself

THE LAST PRONOUN PITFALL I'll mention is mainly a problem for people of Irish descent (I can say that, because I am one): The non-reflexive "myself".

"Myself" is a word you use when you are both the subject and the object of the action (referred to as "reflexive"):

I dressed myself.

If you're not both the subject and the object, don't use it:

~~***Give it to myself when you're finished.~~

As with any other rule, it's fine to break this one in dialog if that's what the person would say.

Negatives

DOUBLE NEGATIVES OF the form "I didn't see none!" or "Ain't nobody got time for that!" mark the speaker as having a low-status dialect. Logically, of course, a double negative makes a positive, but that's not how English usage treats them in this kind of sentence. Instead, they are used for emphasis, adding to one another rather than cancelling each other out. They are fine in dialog if that's what the character would say.

There are also different ways of signalling a negative: the prefix "in-" or "un-" or the word "not". People sometimes combine these in one phrase, such as "not inconceivable".

In narrative, and in general, it's best to avoid having more than two negatives (ideally, avoid more than one), because it will act as a speed bump for your reader while they count the negatives and figure out what you're actually trying to say. Worse than that, once you pass two negatives it's very easy to mess it up and end up with a phrase that says the opposite of what you mean. Take this example:

~~it is not inconceivable that we wouldn't have~~

The first two negatives (not inconceivable) do cancel out, and mean the same as "it's conceivable". The problem here is that the author meant "it's conceivable that we would have," so the extra negative flips the meaning of the sentence. In Old English, that sentence would have been fine, since the rule there was that if you had a negative in a sentence you made as many words as possible negative, and the construction "neither... nor" is a survival of that rule. But in modern English, that sentence says the opposite of what the author intended to say.

It's best to avoid the "not un-" construction completely, unless you're using it to characterize someone who's ponderous and pompous and hedges a lot, rather than committing to a definite statement like "it's conceivable".

Chapter 10: Research and Knowledge

"Research" is the term I'm using for everything that's not story skills (like characterisation or plotting) or mechanical issues (like punctuation and typos). Getting your research wrong is distracting to a knowledgeable reader. Getting it right is often relatively easy.

I am a shockingly superficial researcher. I assume that if I can't find an answer in five or ten minutes on Google, very few people will notice if I just make up something plausible.

On the other hand, if I *can* find it in five or ten minutes on Google, I certainly should.

Some authors love in-depth research. They're very good at it, and it enriches their stories. But there's such a thing as over-enrichment. Don't make your readers drink from the bucket, and certainly don't make them chew on the rope, just because you're drawing from a deep well. (The Turkey City Lexicon, a collection of terms for common writing issues, refers to this one as "I suffered for my art, and now it's your turn.") Don't cram every bit of research into your story until it chokes the plot. Stick to what's relevant or outstandingly cool, and leave the merely interesting in your notebook.

If there's something you want to feature centrally in your story, rather than peripherally, see if you can find an expert, or a forum of enthusiasts. This generally isn't hard, and may prevent you from making embarrassing mistakes. For example, if your main character is a young person who loves science, and knows more about it than you do, find a scientist to check your work so that you don't refer to "charm" as a subatomic particle (it's a characteristic of certain subatomic particles).

Things you should get experts to look over include, by the way, the experiences of groups of people that you don't belong to. Different people experience life differently, which is why we like to read about them. People like to read about themselves, too—but not about ignorant caricatures of themselves. Yes, you may still get some things wrong, but make the effort to get them as right as possible.

The Fiction/Fantasy/Worldbuilding Defense

I post my reviews on Goodreads, and sometimes, when I've pointed out the kind of errors I'm going to talk about in this chapter, a fan of the book will comment on the review and chide me. "Don't you know it's fiction?" "It's fantasy." "It's *worldbuilding*."

The argument appears to be that since this is fiction, or (as it often is, in my case) fantasy fiction, anything goes. The author doesn't have to be knowledgeable about how things work in the real world, or conform in any way to the expectations (or logic) of the real world, because their book isn't set in the real world—or, if it is, it's fiction, so they can make up whatever they like.

I have a firm policy of not engaging in arguments on the internet, so I don't reply to these comments (though I do sometimes report the ones that get personal about my character and ethics, based on the fact that I've given their favourite author an unfavourable review, illustrated with examples of what didn't work for me). But I do want to lay out here a counter to their arguments.

The podcast Writing Excuses presents it in terms of "buy-in" (https://writingexcuses.com/14-37-outlandish-impossibilities/). Your reader has a certain "budget" for buying into your fiction. If they're a speculative fiction reader—fantasy, science fiction, supernatural horror—that budget is probably a bit larger, but every genre requires a certain amount of buy-in. A cozy mystery is not an accurate representation of how real crimes are solved, or even committed. A romance novel is seldom an accurate reflection of how real-life relationships work. A spy thriller usually doesn't reflect the realities of real-life espionage, and so forth. There's a certain amount of buy-in inherent to fiction: not only are you pretending, along with the author, that made-up people exist and are doing imaginary things, but you're also buying into the tropes of the genre (of which more later).

The point the Writing Excuses crew makes in their podcast, and that I want to echo, is that you shouldn't ask your reader to overspend their buy-in budget by dropping things into your fiction that differ significantly from the real world, but are not essential to the genre or to the particular world and story you are creating.

This was expressed by H.G. Wells in a form that is now known as "Wells' Law":

"As soon as the magic trick has been done the whole business of the fantasy writer is to keep everything else human and real. Touches of prosaic detail are imperative and a rigorous adherence to the hypothesis. Any extra fantasy outside the cardinal assumption immediately gives a touch of irresponsible silliness to the invention."

Or, putting it less ponderously, anything that isn't part of the *necessary counterfactual* to make your story work should be as accurate to the real world as you can manage. If you don't adhere to realism in the places where it's not essential for your world to be different, it asks too much buy-in from the reader, too much suspension of disbelief, and risks throwing them out of their immersion in your story.

So, to take a particular example where a fan claimed that my criticism of a book was "mooted" (her word) by the fact that the book was fantasy: believing that a present-day woman time-travelled back to early medieval Wales was part of the necessary counterfactual, without which the story couldn't happen, so I had no problem with that. What I had a problem with was that she insisted to her love interest, the prince, that the "state" should educate its children. My objection was that early medieval Wales had nothing resembling a "state" in the modern sense, and no printing to provide textbooks for the children to learn to read with (or other books for them to read once they had learned how to), and no necessity for them to be able to read in general; that part, in Wells' words, gave "a touch of irresponsible silliness to the invention" and revealed to me that the author hadn't thought it through. (The heroine would have been better off teaching the early medieval Welsh people better sanitation and improving their agriculture, but she, and the author, probably didn't know how to do that.)

Now, clearly these things don't bother every reader, or these fans wouldn't scold me for bringing them up—just as incorrect punctuation, or using the wrong word for what you mean, or tortuous sentences that don't make sense don't bother every reader either. As an author, you have a decision to make. Do I produce the best book I possibly can, that will be admired and enjoyed by knowledgeable readers as well, or do I shoot just for the readers who don't know how to write a sentence or how things work in the real world?

I assume, by the fact that you've picked up this book, that your answer is that you want to make your book as good as it can be. Let's see if I can help you with that.

Names, Titles and Ranks

I don't know about you, but I've more than once had the experience of reading a novel set in a particular time period and getting no authentic sense of that period from the text.

I'm not just talking about the Middle Ages here, either (though that too), but about the 1950s, or the 1930s, or the 1890s. And once I start to analyse the reasons for the lack of that sense of authenticity, it comes down to this: *the text tells me a lot more about the time in which the author grew up, or currently lives, than it does about the time period it's supposedly set in.*

What I mean is that the slang, the cultural references, the attitudes of the characters, the way gender interactions play out, and even the characters' names come from, say, the 1970s or 1980s, or today, rather than from the setting. To me, this is just as bad as making errors in conveying a sense of place. It reduces the richness of the reading experience.

A lot of people don't care, of course, because they don't know, any more than the author does. But *I* care, and so do enough other people that I think it's worth getting right—and getting it right is easier now than at any previous time in history.

Unless you confine your stories to the present day and your own familiar locations and culture (which is a perfectly feasible thing to do), you'll need to do some research if you want your story to feel credible. Technology is an obvious area where stories often trip up—I read a book recently set in World War II which mentioned duct tape, an invention of the 1970s. Fashions and cultural references are another. A book set in the 1930s that mentions a "cheerleader skirt," meaning the kind of short skirt that cheerleaders started wearing in the 1970s, fails to convey a sense of its time. You can check these things on Google and Wikipedia very quickly, if you take a moment to think about them.

I'd like to talk specifically about researching names and words, both because they're something that authors often get wrong when setting their stories in an earlier or other time and place, and because they're easy to get right with a couple of simple tools.

Names

NAMES ARE POWERFUL, not in the fantasy sense of "if the fairy knows your true name they can control you," but in the sense that they convey a place and time. It's worth putting in some effort with your choice of names, because it's a shorthand way to communicate a sense of authenticity—or, if you get it wrong, inauthenticity.

For example, I read a book set in the 1930s (the cheerleader-skirt one, as it happens) in which two of the characters were named Jason and Samantha. Now, it's possible that there were people with those names in the 1930s, but they would have been very unusual, since both names were rare until they became popular in the 1960s. The author, who is my age—so, born in the late 1960s—probably grew up knowing several people with each name, and stuck them into his 1930s story without thinking—and his lack of thought shows.

Likewise, I read a book set in Boston around the time of the American revolution which featured a young woman named Jennifer. Again, this name did exist at the time, but it was almost completely confined to the British county of Cornwall.

Jennifer was the most popular female name in the US for nearly a decade and a half, starting in 1970. No doubt when the author was looking for a name for his young woman character, "Jennifer" sprang to mind almost immediately. To his children, though, it won't be a young woman's name, but a name their mother's friends have. And to their children, it'll be an old lady's name, the equivalent of "Mabel" or "Doris" to my generation (two names that were extremely popular until a sudden decline in the middle of the 20th century). What's more, to someone in 18th-century Boston, it would be rare and exotic.

Fashions in names, especially female names, do change significantly over generations. A British colleague of mine who's about my age once told me that his mother's name, Carol—a common name in her generation, and not that uncommon in ours—had not been given to a single British baby in a recent year.

Some names do go out of fashion and then eventually come back again. My grandmothers' names were Marion and Hazel, both of which (in my country, at least) also weren't given to children for most of the late 20th century, but I've recently started encountering a few young women with those names.

There's also been a growing trend since approximately the 1960s to give girls surnames as first names, a practice that used to be largely confined to boys' names. It may have been accelerated by "Madison", the name taken by Daryl Hannah's character in the 1984 movie Splash, based on a street sign—but "Daryl" itself is also more often considered a male name, and Hannah was born in 1960. (Consider also Cameron Diaz, born 1972.) It's now unremarkable to call a female character Riley or Addison or Darcy or even Ryan, but it would have been highly unusual in an earlier generation.

(There was also a trend for a while in YA and New Adult books to have a female main character with a nickname like Harry or Bill or Ned or something else that sounded masculine, which I never understood. It seemed like a bait-and-switch attempt; your blurb would start out with a masculine name and you'd wait until the second or third sentence to use a pronoun and reveal that Harry (or whoever) was female. The trend appears to have died out as quickly as it sprang up, though.)

The point is: if you're writing fiction set in a period before your adulthood and name your characters, particularly your female characters, based on the names of people you grew up with, you will almost certainly commit an anachronism that will be glaringly obvious to anyone with more historical perspective (such as anyone older than you).

Some names are also characteristic of particular countries. If you meet a Gemma, the likelihood that she was born in Britain is very high. A Skyler is most likely American. (I once came across a blurb for a novel that started out in early medieval Normandy with a character named Skyler. I didn't pick it up, assuming that an author who didn't realize that "Skyler" was a distinctively American name that originated in the 19th century would not do a great job with history in general.)

In an early draft of this chapter, I joked that somewhere there is probably a millennial writing a steampunk novel set in the 1850s featuring protagonists named Kyle and Madison. I cut the joke out as too mean, but since then I've read a story featuring young women in the 1940s named Courtney and Madison, which didn't became popular girls' names until the 1980s. I've also read a novel set in the 1730s with a minor female character named Aubrey, which has only been a girl's name since the 1970s, mainly in the US, and wasn't even revived as a boy's name until the 19th century, having been previously used in the Middle Ages. I've seen it used again for a little French girl in the early 20th century in another book. (She was also carrying a backpack, which wasn't a thing children did until the 1950s.)

How do you get this kind of thing right? It's very simple. The website behindthename.com[1] is only one (but, I think, the most useful one) of a number of websites which trace the rising and falling popularity of first names. The best information is for the US, but other countries are also represented.

This brings me to a pet peeve of mine: fantasy novels in which Christianity and Judaism explicitly don't exist, and yet people are called things like Isaac and Maria. It annoys me not for religious reasons, but because it tells me that the author lacks an awareness of culture and history and hasn't thought things through, which instantly lowers my expectations for the book.

Did you know that biblical names weren't even used in England until after the Norman Conquest (1066)? The Saxons who lived there were Christianised, but they still named their children things like Battle, Elf-Counsel, Noble Bright and Wealth-Guard (that's Hilda, Alfred, Albert and Edward to you). The conquerors brought the practice of using biblical names like John and Peter, but also plenty of non-biblical names like William, Henry, Geoffrey and Alice. And then there were the names adopted from Latin and Greek, often saints' names, though not originally Christian: Phoebe, Claire, Nicholas, George, Julia. Of the 36 kings who have reigned in England since 1066, only four (two Jameses, a John and a Stephen) have had biblical names, though among the six reigning queens who were crowned there have been two Marys, two Elizabeths and an Anne, making five biblically-named queens out of six. (Victoria is the odd woman out.)

---

1. http://behindthename.com/

My point is that it's quite possible to use names that your readers find familiar and can remember without drawing on a cultural heritage that doesn't exist in your setting. (For an example of doing it right, see Sylvia Izzo Hunter's *Noctis Magicae* or *Midnight Queen* trilogy.) And using familiar names is a good way to avoid made-up names that are hard to remember—and sometimes unpronounceable without gargling. If you find yourself spelling a name with apostrophes, and your character is not from the Pacific Islands or certain parts of Africa, stop and think hard about whether you want to commit that particular fantasy cliché.

Check the spelling of your character names, too. I once read a book in which the main character's name was spelled wrong four times, despite the fact that *the book's title included his name, and the other word in the title was spelled almost the same way*, and it had allegedly been past an editor. I've read a short story in which the name of an actual historical person from the 20th century was spelled three different ways inside a few thousand words. Spellcheck won't always catch instances when you've spelled a character's name wrong, especially if your intended spelling is unusual and your typo is the more common spelling, so keep an eye out.

One name I see spelled incorrectly a lot is Jonathan. The second part of it is the same, originally, as the name Nathan. It is not —traditionally, at least—spelled "~~Jonathon~~".

Be very careful with names ending in -an or -on in general. I have seen, for example, ~~Maximillion~~ instead of Maximillian. A lot of Latin-based names end in -an, but are sometimes misspelled with an -on.

Also, watch -ian versus -an. My own surname, McMillan, is frequently given an extra "i" before the "-an" by people who don't know how to spell it, even though there's no "i" in the way it's pronounced.

Finally, there's an important distinction between Francis (a man's name) and Frances (a woman's name).

Male and female names are becoming less distinct in the 21st century, as I've already noted. But especially if you are writing in a historical period, part of your research is checking on what are typical names for the time, and spelling them correctly.

I'm also thinking of a book set shortly after World War II with a character named Will. Between, say, 1920 and 1960, a person named William was substantially more likely to be called Bill rather than Will; it's now closer to even, but I suspect that the Bills are mostly older than the Wills. Bob versus Rob is not so clear-cut, and nor is Jim versus James, but both are trends I've noticed in how people my age and younger are referred to; a young person is more likely to be a Rob or a James than a Bob or a Jim, at least in general English-speaking culture, though there may still be areas where Bob and Jim are preferred. A Richard is more likely to be called Rich than Dick, though there might be other reasons for that.

Specific to fantasy, watch out for what the website TV Tropes refers to as "Aerith and Bob," in which you randomly mix made-up fantasy names with names from our world without any scheme or logic.

In general, think about the names you're using, where they come from, and what they convey.

Titles

I READ A LOT OF FANTASY fiction, which tends to have medieval people in it, and they often have royal or noble titles. I frequently see the titles handled incorrectly. Even more so in steampunk, gaslight fantasy, and Regency romance, which are often set in 19th-century Britain, and so have more of a requirement to conform properly to actual 19th-century British usage than a fantasy novel set in a completely made-up world. In a made-up world, you can at least argue that the conventions are different; I've seen that defense offered of a book I criticized for getting these things wrong. Specifically, I was mainly criticising the misuse of the word "royal" for members of the nobility who were not members of the monarch's family, and the reference to every noble's domain as a "kingdom," which I would argue is a criticism about not knowing the meaning of words, not about ignoring our world's conventions. But: "It's part of the worldbuilding! The author can make up their own rules!" said a fan (paraphrased). Given that none of the other worldbuilding showed any originality, and that the author made multiple other errors, I doubt that this is what was happening; I think she was just making common mistakes because she didn't know any better. After reading what follows, you will know better.

I'm going to lay it out in text first, and then give you a handy table for quick reference.

A king or queen is "Your Majesty". A prince or princess is "Your Highness". (Not the other way around, and I've seen both of them swapped over by multiple authors.) A duke is "Your Grace", and anyone else with a title of nobility—a count (or, in Britain, earl), a viscount, a marquis, or a baron—is usually "My Lord". They don't typically get addressed by the name of their title (dukes and duchesses being exceptions). Then-Prince Charles has been known to joke that when he was in America and people addressed him as "Prince" he felt like one of the Air Force mascot dogs.

As I mentioned above, there is a difference between royalty and nobility; many people, particularly but not solely Americans, confuse the two. If there is any chance that you or your children could legitimately inherit the throne (that is, without raising a rebel army and taking it), you are royal. Otherwise, you are *not* royal. If you have a title of nobility or are closely related to someone with a title of nobility, you are noble, but not royal, unless you are also very closely related to someone with a royal title (king, queen, prince, or princess).

Someone who holds a title will usually be referred to by that title rather than their surname; the Duke of Wellington is Lord Wellington, though his surname is Wellesley. The wife of a holder of a title is Lady Title (not Lady Surname or Lady Firstname Surname).

The son or daughter of a holder of a noble title is not automatically "Lord" or "Lady" themselves, nor are they correctly referred to as peers (only the holders of titles are peers). In current British usage (since the 19th century), the younger sons of dukes and marquesses are Lord Firstname Surname (not Lord Title, since that's their father), but the younger sons of earls, viscounts, or barons are styled (referred to as) the Honourable Firstname Surname and addressed as Mr Surname. For daughters, the cut-off point is different; daughters of dukes, marquesses and earls are all Lady Firstname Surname, but the daughters of viscounts or barons are styled the Honourable Firstname Surname and addressed as Miss Surname. Married noblewomen change their surname but keep their form of address, unless their husband holds a higher rank than their father, in which case their form of address is based on that of the husband.

The eldest son of a duke or earl often has a courtesy title (one of his father's spare titles) that makes him Lord Sparetitle rather than Lord Surname. Sometimes there are enough spare titles that the eldest son's eldest son also gets one. Spare titles happen when a person gets multiple titles from different countries, or different generations of a family are given different higher titles while retaining the lower ones, or when the holder of a title marries a woman who is an heiress (she can't hold the title in her own right, and has no brothers to inherit it, but can transmit it to her sons), or when several people in a family are granted noble titles and one of them doesn't have descendants who qualify to inherit the title, so that title switches over to a cousin who already has a title. The senior person will always use the most senior title, so you could have a duke whose son is a (courtesy) earl, and whose grandson is a (courtesy) viscount. The holders of courtesy titles are not counted as peers, and they do not qualify to sit in the House of Lords. That is, they never did qualify, even before the late-20th-century changes in the rules about who could sit in the House of Lords reduced the number of hereditary peers who could do so.

The Duke of Wellington is a real-life example. In all, the Duke of Wellington has the right to 14 different titles in the peerages of the United Kingdom, Ireland, Spain, Portugal and the Netherlands, which include one Prince, three Dukes, three Marquesses, two Earls, a Count, two Viscounts and two Barons, so there are plenty of spare titles to go round. Governments in Western Europe (outside France, obviously) greatly appreciated the role the original Duke of Wellington played in defeating Napoleon.

The current holder of the title is Charles Wellesley, 9th Duke of Wellington, addressed as Lord Wellington. His son and heir is Arthur Wellesley, who is by courtesy the Earl of Mornington and addressed as Lord Mornington. The original Duke of Wellington was the third son of the first Earl of Mornington (making his style originally the Honourable Arthur Wellesley, before he was made a duke), and because of various people not having children the titles both ended up in the same line in 1863. Earl of Mornington is now a courtesy title. It's usually used by the heir of the Marquess of Douro, who is usually the Duke of Wellington's heir, but in this case, the current Earl of Mornington assumed that title while his father was still Marquess of Douro and has kept it.

The Duke of Wellington's younger son is Lord Fredrick Wellesley, who holds no specific noble title but is "Lord" because he's the son of a duke. The same is true of the current duke's three brothers, Lord Richard Wellesley, Lord John Wellesley and Lord James Wellesley. Lord John Wellesley's son is Mr. Gerald Wellesley.

The current duke's sister is Lady Jane Wellesley, and his daughters are Lady Honor, Lady Mary and Lady Charlotte.

The Earl of Mornington's two sons are Arthur Wellesley, Viscount Wellesley (another courtesy title) and the Honourable Alfred Wellesley, who you would address as Mr. Wellesley. Arthur's twin is Lady Mae Wellesley, because she's the daughter of an earl, even if he's an earl by courtesy.

In the first Lord Peter Wimsey novel by Dorothy L. Sayers, Lord Peter is addressed as "Lord Wimsey" by an American, and quickly corrects him: "No, that's my brother, Denver." (His brother is Gerald Wimsey, Duke of Denver.) Later in the series, he marries, and his wife is both referred to and addressed as "Lady Peter". I suspect that practice may have changed in more recent times, just as we wouldn't refer to a commoner's wife as "Mrs John Smith" these days; married women get to have their own identities now. But for the Wimsey novels, set and written in the 1930s, that was the correct usage.

A knight or baronet is addressed, and referred to, as "Sir Firstname," or referred to as "Sir Firstname Surname". He is *never, ever* correctly referred to or addressed as ***"~~Sir Surname~~," a mistake I've seen in more than one published story—including a traditionally-published novel by an author with a degree in medieval history, who should definitely have known better. Also, a baronet, though some consider him lesser nobility, is not a lord, not a peer (he does not qualify to sit in the House of Lords, and can be elected to the House of Commons without giving up his title), and absolutely not a baron, all of which are things I have seen baronets referred to as in fiction. He's a holder of a hereditary title that lets him call himself "Sir Firstname," like a knight. The difference between a knight and a baronet is that a knight has been given the title in his own lifetime, and it only lasts until his death, but a baronet may have inherited it, and will pass it on to his male heirs. (Moves are afoot in Britain to allow women to inherit baronetcies, but at the time of writing it's still men only.) Baronets are also never "~~Sir Surname~~".

A dame (the female equivalent of a knight) is "Dame Firstname Surname" or "Dame Firstname". Again, she is never **"~~Dame Surname~~".

The wife of a knight or baronet is "Lady Surname." If her husband dies and her son marries, she will become "Firstname, Lady Surname" to distinguish her from her son's wife, who will be "Lady Surname", and likewise if she and her husband divorce and he remarries but she does not, she will be "Firstname, Lady Surname" to distinguish her from the current wife, "Lady Surname". She is *not* correctly referred to as Lady Firstname Surname, since this would indicate that she was the daughter of a duke, marquess, or earl. (Unless she is one of those, of course; in some of the P.G. Wodehouse books we see daughters of earls who married baronets, and they are Lady Firstname Surname.) So a couple of whom the husband is a knight or baronet is referred to as Sir John and Lady Smith, for example.

Here's a handy table for you, in descending order of rank.

Rank	Referred to as	Addressed as	Royal?	Noble?
King or queen	King/Queen Firstname	Your Majesty; Sir/Ma'am; King/Queen Firstname	Yes	
Prince or princess	Prince/Princess Firstname	Your Highness; Sir/Ma'am; Prince/Princess Firstname	Yes	
Duke or duchess	Lord/Lady Title; the Duke/Duchess of Title	Your Grace; Duke/Duchess	No*	Yes
Sons of a duke (with no title)	Lord Firstname Surname	My Lord; Lord Firstname	No	Yes
Daughters of a duke	Lady Firstname Surname	My Lady; Lady Firstname	No	Yes
Marquess or marchioness	Lord/Lady Title; the Marquess/Marchioness of Title	My Lord/Lady; Your Lordship/Ladyship (unless a courtesy title); Lord/Lady Title	No*	Yes
Sons of a marquess (with no title)	Lord Firstname Surname	My Lord; Lord Firstname	No	Yes
Daughters of a marquess	Lady Firstname Surname	My Lady; Lady Firstname	No	Yes
Earl or	Lord/Lady	My Lord/Lady; Your	No*	Yes

Rank	Referred to as	Addressed as	Royal?	Noble?
countess**	Title; the Earl/Countess of Title	Lordship/Ladyship (unless a courtesy title); Lord/Lady Title		
Sons of an earl (with no title)	The Honourable Firstname Surname	Mr Surname	No	Yes
Daughters of an earl	Lady Firstname Surname	My Lady; Lady Firstname	No	Yes
Viscount or viscountess	Lord/Lady Title; the Viscount/Viscountess of Title	My Lord/Lady; Your Lordship/Ladyship (unless a courtesy title); Lord/Lady Title	No	Yes
Sons of a viscount (with no title)	The Honourable Firstname Surname	Mr Surname	No	Yes
Daughters of a viscount	The Honourable Firstname Surname	Miss Surname	No	Yes
Baron or baroness	Lord/Lady Title; the Baron/Baroness of Title	My Lord/Lady; Your Lordship/Ladyship (unless a courtesy title); Lord/Lady Title	No	Yes
Sons of a baron	The Honourable	Mr Surname	No	Yes

Rank	Referred to as	Addressed as	Royal?	Noble?
Daughters of a baron	Firstname Surname The Honourable Firstname Surname	Miss Surname	No	Yes
Baronet	Sir Firstname Surname	Sir Firstname	No	?
Wife of a baronet	Lady Surname	Lady Surname	No	No
Knight	Sir Firstname Surname	Sir Firstname	No	No
Wife of a knight	Lady Surname	Lady Surname	No	No
Dame	Dame Firstname Surname	Dame Firstname	No	No

Notes:

*Some people who are royal (closely related to the monarch) hold noble titles as well, but holding a noble title does not make a person royal.

**A note on why an earl's wife is a countess. The word *eorl* in Old English means a nobleman or chieftain, and after the Norman Conquest it was kept as a noble title. It's the equivalent of the rank which is referred to as "count" in English when it's conferred by a non-British monarch, although none of the European languages use this exact word. It's related to the territorial designation "county".

If you're going to include title-holders in your fiction, take the time to check into how they should be referred to and addressed. The Wikipedia article on Royal and Noble Styles[2] is a good starting point, but consider people like bishops, ambassadors and so forth as well. Part of giving a sense of time and place in your story is getting things like this right.

The usage differed from country to country and changed at different periods, of course. Medieval British kings, for example, were "Your Grace". But unless you're writing fiction set in a real place and time in our world that isn't post-18th-century Britain, if you stick with current British usage you'll probably be all right. Like anything involving years of tradition, there are conventions that don't necessarily make a lot of sense (like the cut-off for sons being "Lord" being set at a different level than the cut-off for daughters being "Lady"); looking them up is the only way to be sure you're getting it right. You'll get a bit more slack in a completely made-up setting than you will in a fantastical or science-fictional version of our own world, but if you do things in such a setting that are visually indistinguishable from common mistakes a lot of people make out of ignorance, people who do know the rules will assume you don't know the rules.

While we're on the subject of titles, a subtle point about the numbering of monarchs (and popes, who get numbers under similar circumstances). I recently read a book set in the Regency period (early 19th century) that referred to "Queen Elizabeth I". However, as I was reminded by an annotation on a story by P.G. Wodehouse from the early 20th century, until the reign of Queen Elizabeth II began in 1952, Elizabeth Tudor was just "Queen Elizabeth". In the same way, since there's only been one King John of England, he's simply King John; nobody calls him "John I" because there's no John

---

II yet. This is similar to the more obvious case of World War I/the First World War; it wasn't called that until the Second World War came along. Prior to that it was usually called the Great War, though Francis A. March did publish a *History of the World War* starting in 1918.

To really get into the mindset of an earlier period and look at things the way people of that period looked at them is challenging, and I don't blame the author concerned for making the mistake of referring to "Elizabeth I" before there was an Elizabeth II, but now you've been reminded and can avoid making the same mistake yourself.

Further on terms of address outside the nobility: In Britain until relatively recently, and possibly still today in some circles, there were strict unspoken rules about how you addressed another person, similar to those which are still observed in Japan. Note that in the following I will follow the British convention that a title like "Mr" doesn't require a period/full stop after it if it ends with the last letter of the full title; in American English, the period is always required.

The following are generalizations applying, to varying degrees, in the period from about the late 18th century up to about World War II, but mainly to the 19th and early 20th centuries.

Men who had been to public school or belonged to the "gentry" or the professions (doctor, lawyer, etc.) would almost invariably address one another by their surnames, though they might add a "Mr" if they didn't know each other well or had just met. I started reading a book once in which the characters, who introduced themselves as Jack, Ronald and Charles, were very obviously meant to be the Inklings (C.S. "Jack" Lewis, John Ronald Reuel Tolkien and Charles Williams) in their youth having an adventure in another world; but those men would never have introduced themselves to strangers by their first names without surnames, and, indeed, when they actually were close friends they addressed each other by their surnames as a matter of course (except that Lewis called Tolkien "Tollers" as a nickname). Holmes and Watson never called each other Sherlock and John, despite being close associates for years.

On the other hand, Bertie Wooster and his friends in P.G. Wodehouse, who mostly belong to the same private club, the Drones Club, all address each other by nicknames or, occasionally, first names (Bertie is one of the few without a nickname, though since his full name is Bertram, Bertie is a kind of nickname); this underlines what frivolous youths they all are, though it may also reflect the start of a shift, since the Wodehouse books are all implicitly set in the period between the two World Wars, when he started publishing his most popular works. Many of the Drones were also at school together, which might create a bond close enough to justify using a first name, though boys were usually addressed by their surnames by masters and other boys alike. If several boys (usually from the same family) had the same surname, the oldest would be known as Surname Major, the younger brother as Surname Minor, and, if there was a third brother, the youngest would be Surname Minimus. Girls at school, in contrast, were known as Miss Surname to teachers, and usually by first name to their classmates.

Men of this class would address women of their own class as Mrs or Miss Surname unless they were their sisters, cousins, unusually close friends, or accepted romantic partners, in which case they would use their first names. One of Wodehouse's short stories in the collection *Meet Mr Mulliner* includes a declaration of love that begins, "Miss Blake—Susan—" as the would-be lover dares to claim the intimacy of the first name of the woman he's about to ask to marry him.

Women of the upper and upper-middle class would address their male and female acquaintances with the appropriate title (Mr, Mrs, Miss, Dr, Professor, Major) prefixed, or by a professional title like Doctor, Professor or Major, but would call their close friends by their first names. Miss Jane Marple, for example, in the Agatha Christie books, is Miss Marple to everyone except her many young relatives and godchildren, who call her Aunt Jane, and her few close female friends, who call her Jane.

In the Regency period at least (early 19th century), there was a convention that the oldest unmarried daughter of a gentry family was "Miss Surname" and her younger sisters were "Miss Firstname Surname"; when the eldest daughter married, the next daughter then became "Miss Surname". This practice continued at least into the Victorian era, and I have seen an example of it in a book published as late as 1919 (J.S. Fletcher's *The Middle Temple Murder*).

Members of the lower middle class mostly went by their surname with a title prefixed among themselves, and it wasn't uncommon for married couples to continue to call each other "Mr Surname" and "Mrs Surname" even in private in the 18th and 19th centuries. Close friends or colleagues might call each other by their first names.

Servants had a hierarchy, marked out by how they were addressed. A senior male servant such as a butler or valet or a head gardener would be addressed by his employer (and any other person of his employer's class who found it necessary to address him) by surname only, hence "Jeeves," but among themselves, the servants would address senior male servants as "Mr Surname".

A senior female servant such as a housekeeper or cook would often, by convention, be "Mrs Surname" to everyone, whether or not she was married. Junior servants such as footmen or housemaids would be addressed by first names, though ladies' maids who acted as the female equivalent of a valet would be addressed by surname.

As an aside, E.S. Turner's book *What the Butler Saw: Two Hundred and Fifty Years of the Servant Problem* claims (as quoted on the P.G. Woodhouse annotation site madameulalie.org, in the annotations for *Leave It To Psmith*) that 'The footman was addressed by his Christian name, or rather by *a* Christian name, not necessarily his own. The most usual names were Charles, James, John and John Thomas . . .' The claim is that some employers didn't bother to learn the names of their junior staff (both male and female) and so assigned them conventional names, which were inherited when the staff changed over. I haven't been able to find any other source confirming this, however, which suggests that if the practice existed at all, it was not widespread or at least not universal, and I haven't come across a clear example of it in fiction, either, though I don't read a lot of fiction written in the 19th century. Still, you could use it if you wanted. Footman names do seem to mostly follow a pattern, at least in fiction I've read; apart from Thomas, Andrew and Robert, they are mostly drawn from the nine names that English kings have used since the Norman Conquest, namely Charles, James, Henry, William, John, George, and (less likely) Stephen, Edward and Richard. The best-known fictional footman, however, is probably Joseph Andrews, in the 1742 novel of the same name by Henry Fielding. His employers called him Joseph.

Governesses, who were usually women of "good breeding" whose family circumstances made it necessary for them to earn a living by teaching other people's children (in the family home, before the early-teenage boys went to boarding school or the late-teenage girls went to finishing school), would often be the only members of staff who got a "Miss" before their surnames.

As an aside, governess or else lady's companion (a paid position, though not usually well-paid, and at least in theory absolutely not a servant) were about the only respectable employment options open to an unmarried upper-class woman whose family had fallen on hard times in the 19th century. As higher education for women became more common from the late 19th century onwards, they could also become schoolteachers or run private girls' schools. Making a living by writing could also be respectable, depending on what one wrote. Naturally, there were plenty of young women of all classes, married and unmarried, who did things that they weren't supposed to and that weren't considered respectable, either openly or covertly. A transition which the two World Wars accelerated allowed women of all classes to be employed in an ever-widening range of occupations. Women of the lower-middle and middle classes, of course, had been working at many occupations, usually unpleasant and poorly paid ones, for a long time before this.

Returning to servants and terms of address: Servants would address their employers and their employers' family members as sir, madam, or miss, depending on their gender and marital status; they would refer to the members of the household by whatever their correct title was, except that the children of the family would be "Mr Firstname" or "Miss Firstname" (or, in the case of married women, "Mrs Surname"), unless they were entitled to be called something else such as "Lord Firstname," since calling them all by their father's surname wouldn't distinguish them adequately.

Members of the lower classes who were not servants would typically be addressed by members of the upper classes by their surnames; by members of the middle class by their title and surname; and by fellow members of the lower class by title and surname to indicate respect and distance, or by first name if they were friends or had known each other a long time. A woman might refer to her husband in the third person by his surname alone.

In general, it would be not merely insulting but unthinkable to address someone by their first name without an appropriate degree of intimacy already existing, the more so the higher their rank. In a popular steampunk novel set in the 19th century, a doctor and a duke, during a professional consultation by the doctor, address each other by first name; this would not have happened in reality unless they were extraordinarily close friends, which these two characters were not. On the other hand, Lord Peter Wimsey and his good friend Chief-Inspector Parker often call each other Peter and Charles, indicating the closeness of their relationship even before they became brothers-in-law, though they do also address each other by their surnames at times.

Military Ranks

I CAME ACROSS A BOOK a while ago that gave an ex-RAF officer from World War II the rank of "captain," which is not and has never been an RAF rank. Possibly the author was thinking of "Captain W.E. Johns," author of the Biggles books, who was in the Royal Flying Corps in World War I, when the rank of captain did still exist (but he doesn't ever seem to have actually held it). Or possibly the author was just unaware that the RAF, unlike the USAF, does not use army ranks but has its own rank system—something that you really should know if you are writing a book in which the main character, who insists on her ex-military rank and whose rank is used in the book's title, served in the RAF. (A female RAF officer in World War II is a necessary counterfactual for the story to happen, in this case, but, given how many other errors this particular author made, I'm confident that the rank name issue was simply the result of ignorance, not a deliberate choice with a purpose behind it.)

It used to be the case in Britain that retired military officers sometimes used their former rank as their title in civilian life, instead of "Mr". Technically, I believe this is still permitted to officers of the rank of major or above in the British Army or Royal Marines, lieutenant-commander or above in the British Navy, or squadron leader in the RAF, but in practice not many people do so anymore, and it tends to be considered pretentious unless the context justifies it, such as if you are running a veterans' charity. But almost any British novel set in a small village in the 20th century will have a Major or a Colonel in it somewhere. The bluff ex-military man (who had usually served in India or Africa) is as much a stock character of the English fictional village as the mild-mannered vicar, the skeptical and often Scottish doctor, or the fluffy elderly spinster.

Former army captains also sometimes kept their rank as their title, though even in the 20th century it was often considered pretentious. Also, someone who had left the army with the rank of captain had probably either held a wartime rank and hence not been a career officer (meaning he was not really entitled to keep the rank), or had left the army early in his career, possibly having been discharged for "conduct unbecoming an officer," so calling yourself "Captain Surname" as a civilian could convey not only that you were a bit of a poser but also that you were potentially dodgy or, at least, not very successful. Retired captains in the cavalry were given more latitude in this regard if they continued to work with horses in civilian life, as in the case of Captain Mark Phillips, at one time married to Princess Anne.

The P.G. Wodehouse annotations site madameulalie.org baldly states on its page for *Blandings Castle and Elsewhere*: "In English literature, former army officers who use the rank of Captain are almost always bounders (cf. Trollope's Captain Bellfield, for instance)... Rather like the convention that baronets are always bad, it's probably grossly unfair, but a convenient short-cut for writers." I tend to treat the generalized pronouncements on this particular website as unproven until confirmed with better evidence, however.

The above statement doesn't seem to apply to Captain Arthur Hastings, Hercule Poirot's friend in the Agatha Christie novels, for example. His rank is not mentioned in *The Mysterious Affair at Styles*, in which he first appears (he's always "Mr. Hastings," "Monsieur Hastings" or just "Hastings"), even though it's set during World War I and he is currently a serving officer sent back to England to recover from a wound, but he's introduced, and introduces himself, as "Captain Hastings" in subsequent stories, after he has left the service—even though he says in the first book that he's not a professional soldier, and so only held a wartime commission. He's not very bright, being modelled on Holmes's Watson (also an ex-military man, who left the service because of a wound), but he's certainly not a bounder, being, in fact, brave, loyal, and scrupulous to a fault.

I think the conclusion is that, if you're setting your story in 20th-century Britain, you should use your own judgement about men who use their former military titles.

Consider also that occasionally non-commissioned officers were known by their ranks after their retirement, if they were in an occupation where that former rank was relevant. For example, the Sergeant in Rudyard Kipling's *Stalky & Co* is in charge of discipline at the school which is the book's setting.

Use of Words

It's easy to spot an author who hasn't thought about or researched their vocabulary. The same book set in the 1930s that I've already referenced twice (for the cheerleader skirt and the characters named Jason and Samantha) also used the phrase "warm fuzzies," which I thought everyone knew arose in the 1970s; clearly, I was wrong. There's an excellent tool to avoid this kind of slip-up. It's called Google Ngram Viewer, and it's at: https://books.google.com/ngrams.

Google has digitised millions of books and other documents, going back as far as 1500, and put them into a searchable database which you can use to find when a word or phrase came into use and the trends in its usage. Using more advanced queries, you can see usage of different parts of speech, like "truck" as a noun versus "truck" as a verb (take a look at "About Ngram Viewer," linked at the bottom of the page, for full instructions).

In just a couple of seconds, you can check whether your 1880s steampunk heroine should say "I felt a surge of adrenaline" (she shouldn't; adrenaline wasn't discovered yet).

This is something to watch out for, by the way: we have a lot of common phrases that use medical or psychological jargon (a surge of adrenalin, getting closure, having a complex, being anal...) which may not belong in your historical piece, because they had not been coined yet. We're so used to them that we use them without thinking. To avoid anachronisms, you need to train yourself to think about them.

If the phrase you want to use wasn't in use yet, what do you substitute? If you want to say "freaked out" (1960s) but your story takes place in 1939, you might find this resource useful:

http://www.phrases.org.uk/.

There's also the Historical Dictionary of American Slang at: http://www.alphadictionary.com/slang/.

John Stephen Farmer compiled several works on slang, both British and American, up to the late 19th century. They are now in the public domain.

I've also experimented with ChatGPT and found that it's reasonably good at translating colloquial phrases into earlier versions of English. For example, I gave it the prompt "Translate the phrase 'a surge of adrenalin' into English of the 1850s" and got the response "In English of the 1850s, the phrase 'a surge of adrenaline' might be expressed as 'a rush of vital spirits' or 'a thrilling impulse of the humors.'"

Your results may vary with different phrases, depending how easy it is to match the concepts. For example, I asked ChatGPT to translate "get closure" into English of the 1890s and it suggested "find solace" or "obtain finality," neither of which is particularly close; I would suggest "close the book" as a better translation, but the problem is that "closure" is a piece of psychological jargon for a concept that didn't really exist as a distinct idea prior to its coinage. Sometimes, you just need to be aware that people in earlier times didn't think the same way as we do, and not put ideas in their mouths that don't belong there.

The author Mary Robinette Kowal once went so far as to put all of the words found in Jane Austen's novels into a custom spellcheck dictionary and use it to find instances where she was using anachronistic vocabulary in her novels set in Austen's time. That's probably excessive, on the one hand, and on the other hand won't catch the times you use a word that Austen used, but in a different sense from the modern one—and you will still have some more checking to do, as Kowal did, when you've used a word that was used in Austen's time, just not by her. But it shows an ambition for authenticity that I applaud in general concept.

It's probably better, though, on balance, to strive for an authentic feel conveyed by certain carefully chosen phrases and an avoidance of obvious anachronisms, rather than something that a scholar of the literature of the period would have trouble distinguishing from the real thing. Most readers won't notice the difference between the two—or rather, will notice that the excessively realistic version is harder to read, and contains what they think are errors. For a good example, take a look at Sylvia Izzo Hunter's Midnight Queen trilogy, which to me—not a scholar of Regency literature, but someone who's read some of it and knows roughly what it's like—comes across as conveying an authentic feel of the time, without sacrificing fluency and readability. It does this, in part, by focusing on the dialog as the place to put the period phrases, choosing to make the narrative more neutral without being obviously too modern.

What I've just described is at a high skill level, and most writers won't be able to attain it. What you can do, though, is keep from dropping anachronisms into the middle of your prose that will instantly bounce anyone who knows much about language at all out of your story.

Laying a Lie to Rest?

WHILE WE'RE ON WORDS, let's talk about *lay* versus *lie* as an example of a wider question about when, and when not, to use your own dialect.

In a lot of places that discuss grammar—even a lot of places that normally discuss it from the perspective of "if enough people use it, it's correct usage"—you will find advice that says it's important to make the "correct" choice between the verbs "lay" and "lie". There is a rule, there is a right way and a wrong way, there is a normative practice, and you should not depart from it.

I'm going to take a slightly different approach.

Depending on your dialect of English, you may be more or less likely to say, for example, "I need to lay down" rather than "I need to lie down". Southern US English is probably most given to the first phrasing, followed by other US dialects, but both versions are used in all English dialects that I'm aware of apart from the very highest-status ones. The first version also tends to be most often used by people with less education or from a lower socio-economic class (though, again, educated people from the southern US are more likely to use it than educated people from elsewhere).

And the thing with writing about language and usage is that it's generally educated people from a middle-class-or-higher background who do it, and, no matter how hard we try, humans generally think of what they've grown up doing as "correct" and "right," and things that people less fortunate than themselves do differently as "wrong" and "lesser". There is more than that going on with "lay/lie," as I'll discuss below, but don't for a moment think that that isn't part of what is going on.

What I'm going to do is this. I will describe what is usually considered the "correct" usage. It's what I use myself—I'm an educated speaker of New Zealand English, who grew up in a first-generation middle-class household (both my parents were schoolteachers, but their families of origin were tradespeople and manual workers for many generations back). But then I'll talk about when you might want to use the "incorrect" version—and when you maybe might not want to, even if that's how you usually talk.

A likely part of the reason people sometimes use "lay" where strict usage would prescribe "lie" is that the present tense form of one is the past tense form of the other:

VERB PRESENT TENSE	PAST TENSE
Lie I lie on the bed	I lay on the bed
Lay I lay my money down	I laid my money down

You can see how that would be confusing.

The distinction is that *lie* means *adopt a reclining position*, and it doesn't require an object. *Lay*, on the other hand, means *place*, and it does require an object. You could substitute as follows:

VERB	PRESENT TENSE	PAST TENSE
Recline	I recline on the bed	I reclined on the bed
Lay	I place my money down	I placed my money down

That's straightforward, because "recline" and "place" are both what is known as "regular verbs"; they generate a past tense by adding "-ed" at the end (or actually, since both of them already have the "e", by adding "d"). And, of course, they sound nothing alike.

"Lay" is also a regular verb; the past tense is "laid" (though it does require a spelling change, not just an "-ed" ending). But "lie" is an irregular verb, which changes to the past tense by changing its vowel—and in doing so, it becomes a word that is spelled, and also sounds, exactly like the present tense of "lay".

Probably not helping is the fact that there is a different verb, meaning "to deliberately say something untrue," which is also "lie" in the present tense, but is "lied" in the past tense.

All of this creates a perfect storm of reasons why people might say "I laid down on the bed".

Nor does it stop there. Let's extend our table:

VERB	PRESENT TENSE	PAST TENSE	PRESENT PARTICIPLE	PAST PARTICIPLE
Lie	I lie on the bed	I lay on the bed	I am lying on the bed	I had lain on the bed
Lay	I lay my money down	I laid my money down	I am laying my money down	I had laid my money down

People who say "I laid on the bed" are also likely to say "I am laying on the bed" and "I had laid on the bed".

I would like to propose to you that people who use "lay" in place of "lie" are engaging in a dialectic variation. They are using it consistently, they are declining it consistently (the various tenses follow the same pattern as the "standard" usage of "lay"); they are simply substituting one verb for another similar verb. Whether this started as a mistake or a confusion is not really the point. It's how they talk, and it's no more "incorrect"—for them—than using "spit" as both present and past tense is for people who do that (who are often the same people).

And this is not a new thing, either. Merriam-Webster's note on usage says that "lay" has been used for "lie" since the 14th century, and it's only since about 1770 that people started to make a rule about it.

Let's see, can we think of a major English-speaking nation that was colonized largely before 1770? Hmmm.

The really important thing, however, and what I want to zero in on, is not whether the lay/lie distinction is in any sense objectively "correct English," because there's no such thing; language changes, it's changed by its speakers' usage changing, and English in particular has no gatekeeping body like the Académie Française that issues official pronouncements about the language (not that most French people probably take much notice of their one in any case).

The first important thing to note about conventions like this—because it is a convention—is that some people will notice if you break them, and that will distract them from your story. This is what my whole book is about: learning the conventions so that, by following them, you will cause your mechanics and usage to recede into the background and not be noticed in a negative way by your readers.

The other important thing to note is that the use, or non-use, of a convention like this locates you in a particular part of the dialect space of English. It's a wide and generous space, which takes in English as it is spoken in Scotland, Ireland, India, Singapore, the Caribbean, Canada, Australia, South Africa, and New Zealand as well as in England and the US, and within those locations there are sometimes regional variations, and very often variations based on social class. The reason I mention this is that if you are, say, an American author writing a steampunk story set in 19th-century London with middle-class characters, there are many readers who will get distracted if you substitute "lay" for "lie," because that's not authentic to the dialect of the people you are writing about (however much it may be authentic to your dialect).

To use an analogy, if I am describing a US or British farmer in fiction, I won't put him in a Swanndri, which is a specific brand of heavy bush shirt made from wool in a tartan pattern, and worn almost universally by New Zealand farmers. It's part of my mental image of "farmer," because I grew up in New Zealand, but it would be a mistake to place it anywhere else; farmers outside New Zealand seldom if ever wear Swanndris.

On the other hand, you maybe don't want to try too hard to write a strong dialect you don't personally speak, either. I'm thinking of the absolutely terrible job I saw the well-known SFF author Ann McCaffrey do with two Australian characters, and the equally bad job another author did with my own dialect, New Zealand English, in one of the few stories I've seen with a New Zealand character that wasn't by a New Zealand author. What tends to happen is that someone who doesn't speak the dialect will pull out a few phrases (often ones that are already old-fashioned) that they've heard somehow, and ram them together in a way that, to a native speaker, seems completely artificial and false—and heavy-handed; most people who speak English speak it with a touch of dialect here and there, rather than in a series of dialect phrases piled on top of one another. A heavy dialect draws attention to itself, and it's most likely that you don't want the reader's attention on how well or badly you've done the dialect; you want it to be on what the character is saying and how that contributes to your story. Less is more, with dialect as with so much else.

I've strayed a little way from "lie" vs "lay," but it's in service of my main point, which is: I consider the use of "lay" in place of "lie" to be a legitimate dialectal variation, but it's important that you're aware of it as such, and use the two verbs in your writing in a way that works for the story you're telling and its intended audience, and is correct for the dialect *of the characters*. The same is true of other dialectal variations.

I once had an argument with an author acquaintance on social media whose particular dialect included usages like "that needs changed," where other dialects would use "that needs changing" or "that needs to be changed". This is originally an Irish or Scots usage, but is also used in parts of the US settled from Ireland or Scotland, including, presumably, the part she came from. I have heard it from speakers in New Zealand who come from Southland, another region settled primarily by Scots, as well.

I suggested, when I saw it in her fiction, that because it was a dialect usage, she might want to use the more "standard US English" versions instead. She responded, with some annoyance, that there was no such thing as "standard US English," which is technically correct—I'd phrased it poorly—but also missed my point. In supposed-to-be-neutral third-person narration, or in the narrative voice or dialog of someone who didn't come from the part of the US she came from, that minority-dialect usage stands out, and not in a good way.

Made-Up Rules of English

IN THE 18TH AND 19TH centuries, a few people without enough to do started making up rules of English that they felt *ought* to be true, even though actual usage was against them. Several of these were attempts to make English more like Latin, and most of them were originally personal opinions about what sounded better. Some of these "rules" have, at various times, been taught in schools as if they were real rules of English, and at least one has become widely adopted as a result, though most of them have only been adopted by pedantic people.

These rules fall into several groups: those that are mostly used by pedants and make speakers sound excessively formal; one that is now frequently used, despite being completely made up; and those that definitely mark speakers as speaking a low-status dialect, but are nevertheless completely understandable and have plenty of precedent in high-status written English.

Pedantic Rules

IF YOUR CHARACTER IS an old-fashioned, uptight person with an expensive education, they should not end a sentence with a preposition, begin one with a conjunction, or split their infinitives, all of which are made-up rules that most speakers of English don't observe. But if they was just brung up all anyhow, they can certainly do these things; and for that matter you can do them in narrative, and most people who are not old-fashioned and uptight won't be bothered by it. Shakespeare, I believe, broke all three of these rules, probably because they were invented after his time.

Excessively formal, over-correct speech or writing that observes these rules is marked as unusual, and characterizes the speaker or writer as ponderous.

Ending a Sentence with a Preposition

A preposition, remember, is one of those small words like "to" or "with" or "under" that indicates a relationship between two things in space and time (or, often, more abstractly). There's a made-up rule that's sometimes taught that says you shouldn't put a preposition at the end of a sentence. The reason for this is simply that "preposition" is from a Latin word that indicates that it's positioned before ("pre") something else. Since English isn't descended from Latin, but from a common ancestor with German, in actual English usage a preposition is a perfectly normal thing to end a sentence with. I just did it right there, and you may not have even noticed.

There is a well-known story that Winston Churchill wrote, next to a note on an official memorandum where someone had pointed out that a sentence ended with a preposition, "This is the sort of nonsense up with which I will not put." The convoluted sentence structure vividly makes the point about how unnatural it sounds to twist yourself into knots trying to observe this imaginary rule. Although the attribution to Churchill is almost certainly mythical, the point remains.

Beginning a Sentence with a Conjunction

Conjunctions are the words like "and" or "but" or "because" or "while" which link thoughts together. See the discussion in Sentence Patterns under Pattern 1c: Independent Clause Introduced with Coordinating Conjunction. English speakers and writers have been starting sentences with them for centuries, and most people would be surprised to be told they aren't supposed to.

Splitting an Infinitive

The infinitive in English is the form of the verb that is preceded by "to," like "to go" or "to speak" or "to write". Pedants in the 19th century decided that you shouldn't put anything in between the two parts, even though people had been doing so for centuries. The most famous split infinitive is Star Trek's "to boldly go where no man has gone before," which you can easily rewrite as "to go boldly where no man has gone before." However, the original version puts the emphasis on "go," whereas the rewrite puts it on "boldly"; they are not quite the same.

Nor can you always rewrite easily. The YouTube channel RobWords, which has (at least at time of writing) an excellent video on made-up English rules, gives the example "I would like **to more than double** my subscribers this year," which requires a complete rewrite if you're to find a sentence with the same meaning that doesn't split the infinitive. You would need something like "I would like to increase my subscriber numbers to more than double," which is less natural and wordier. (The second "to" in that sentence is a preposition, not part of an infinitive, if you were wondering.)

Actually Observed Made-Up Rules

I'M ONLY AWARE OF ONE of these. The supposed rule that "less is for mass nouns, fewer is for count nouns" was invented by one grammarian named Baker in 1770, who offered it as a suggestion, not a rule. However, it's been so widely taught and adopted that if you're representing the speech or writing of educated people, particularly in the past, you should probably not say "there were less than ten of them" but "there were fewer than ten of them". It's a rule now in decline in actual usage, though.

It is occasionally ambiguous to use "less" with count nouns, as in the following example:

> We need less bad people to be involved.

Here, there are two possible interpretations, one of which is "We need a smaller number of bad people" and the other of which is "We need people who are less bad". Saying "We need fewer bad people" or "We need better people" is unambiguous.

Made-Up Rules that Mark Class Distinctions

THE BRITISH HAVE TRADITIONALLY made class distinctions extremely important, and so language usages that mark those class distinctions are important too. The clearest example here is the double negative ("Ain't nobody got time for that!"), which I discuss more fully in the Clarity of Reference chapter under Negatives. "Lay" versus "lie," discussed exhaustively above, is another example.

You should go right ahead and speak your own dialect all you want; as long as they can understand you, that's nobody else's business. But be aware of it, especially when writing, and be aware of how it will sound to others, and of whether it will give them a smoother or bumpier reading experience.

Writing Englishes: British and American

WHAT I WAS TALKING about in the previous section got me thinking about the differences between dialects of English. English is usually regarded as a single language, but that's a simplification.

It's spoken as a first language by significant numbers of people who live in England, Ireland, Scotland, Wales, Canada, the USA, various nations in the Caribbean, New Zealand, Australia, Fiji, Samoa, Papua New Guinea, India, Pakistan, Sri Lanka, Singapore, Malaysia, South Africa, Botswana, Nigeria, Ghana, Kenya, and Uganda, to give a distinctly incomplete list. All these people speak it differently from each other, and in several of the places where it's the primary language (Britain and the USA), there are also significant regional and class differences in vocabulary, pronunciation and even grammar.

Of the various forms of English, there are two that have high status as written forms of the language: British English (BrE) and American English (AmE). While, as I've just said, there is no one British English and no one American English as far as the spoken language is concerned, and while there's no central authority that enforces standardization on either form, there are some systematic conventions that are usually observed when writing British English or American English.

British English is also, more or less, the written English of most of the British Commonwealth (countries that belonged to the British Empire before its breakup after World War II). I say "most" because Canada, being next to the USA, uses a hybrid of British English and American English. I'm not Canadian, so I can't say a lot about Canadian English, but because New Zealand—where I'm from—imports books from both Britain and the USA, and also because I was educated in a form of British English but have been married to an American since 1999, I'm more aware than most people of the differences between British and American English.

If you are setting your story in London and use words and phrases like "sidewalk" (rather than "pavement"), "a few blocks away," "had gotten" (rather than "had got"), "she wrote him" (rather than "wrote to him"), "he can come stay" (rather than "come and stay" or "come to stay"), "different than" (rather than "different from") or "off of" (rather than "off"), people who are familiar with the differences between US and British English will be distracted, and their immersion in your story will be broken. My immersion was broken, for example, reading Tim Powers' award-winning book *Declare*, in which the Cambridge-educated, very British viewpoint character constantly says "off of" and occasionally says "sure". If you care about your readers' immersion at all, it's worth finding someone who speaks the dialect in question and asking them to go over your manuscript (it would be best to offer to pay them for this, or exchange a similar favour) and point out moments where your dialect is obtrusive.

Despite my extensive exposure to American English, I still asked a colleague on a writers' forum to check over the parts of one of my books that are written from the point of view of a woman from Boston. (My wife is from California, which is a somewhat different dialect.) I got some things wrong, too, which my colleague pointed out. For example, I had my character say "hands up who thinks that…" and he suggested substituting "show of hands, who thinks that…," since "hands up" in the US is associated with being threatened with a gun, not with indicating your vote.

George Bernard Shaw famously described Britain and the USA as "two nations separated by a common language." While most British and American people are able to make themselves understood to each other with minimal difficulty if they don't use colloquialisms (apart from a few vocabulary items that mean different things on the two sides of the Atlantic—of which more below), there are some common markers which will tell an alert person which dialect you are writing in.

I'm not just talking about the spelling, though certainly that too; American spelling was partially reformed through the efforts of Noah Webster in the 19th century, with *center* replacing *centre* and *color* replacing *colour*, for example, and the endings of words like *organize* using -ize instead of -ise as in British English, while words like *canceled* lose the non-functional double letter in British English *cancelled*. Setting your spellchecker to the appropriate version of English will take care of this for you.

Spelling apart, though, there are ways of phrasing things and frequently-used vocabulary that, to someone who knows the difference, will scream "American" or "British".

This becomes important if you are a speaker of one dialect and your characters are speakers of the other. I most often see the problem with Americans trying to write British people, but it goes the other way as well.

Here are some examples I've noted in published books that I've read, or that are likely to come up often. They are easily avoided if you're aware of them, but if you're unaware, you risk breaking the immersion of your reader by dropping a clanging dialect error into the middle of your narrative. In some cases, I point out that the difference is specific to Britain itself, in which case the American term is usually used in other nations that use British English.

This is a starter list, and you should do your own research, using a historical dictionary if you plan to set your story in the past, to avoid anachronisms.

Phrases

BRE "THE NEXT COUPLE of days" (AmE often or usually omits "of").

AmE "Where is it at?" (BrE omits "at").

AmE "off of" (BrE generally omits "of").

BrE "back to mine" (AmE, English outside Britain, and many British people would say "back to my place"; I've seen this used by a British writer setting his book in the US, though).

BrE "I was sat" (this is, itself, a dialect usage rather than "standard" BrE, which says "I was sitting," the same as AmE).

BrE "I'll go and look" (AmE usually omits "and" between "come" or "go" and another verb).

BrE "I'll see you on Thursday" (AmE often omits "on").

BrE "cobblestoned street" (AmE frequently omits the "d" and says "cobblestone street").

Compare "unbias platform" (claimed by social media platform GETTR) and "close-minded" for "closed-minded". I've also seen "his trouble childhood," but that may be merely a typo. The difference between the ones that are different but valid ("cobblestone street") and the ones that are considered errors ("unbias platform") is that "cobblestone" is what the street is made of, and can therefore work like "stone wall"; as a noun, it can inherently be used to modify another noun without changing its form, in a way that doesn't work for adjectives that are not also nouns.

AmE "she's visiting with her friend" can mean that she is at home and the friend has come to see her; in BrE this would be phrased as "her friend has come to visit her," and the phrase "visit with" is unlikely to occur. In BrE, "visit" implies that the person doing the visiting is not in their home, but in the home of the other party.

BrE "I suppose" vs AmE "I guess". (The American usage is becoming more common in Britain, but the longer ago your story is set, the less likely your British character is to say "I guess" when they mean "I suppose".)

AmE "a ways away"; BrE would probably say "some distance off".

AmE "do you have...?" vs BrE "have you got...?"

AmE "I will" vs BrE "I shall".

A terminological oddity that doesn't belong anywhere else: in BrE, the floor of a building at street level is the ground floor, and the first floor is the floor above that. AmE has a more rational method of calling the street level the first floor and the floor above that the second floor.

Now, specific vocabulary words. Since I more often see American authors getting British English wrong, I will mention the American version first and alphabetize by it. I've also grouped them into themes, so if, for example, you are setting a scene in a kitchen, you can check the "Food and Drink" section.

Entries with the keyword in **bold** are cases where the same word is used in BrE and AmE to mean two different things, rather than two different words being used to mean the same thing, as in the other entries.

This is not a comprehensive list, and you should always do your own checking; the point is to make you aware of some of the commoner differences.

General Vocabulary

AME "AIRPLANE" VS BRE "aeroplane".

AmE "anyplace" vs BrE "anywhere". Also someplace vs somewhere, noplace vs nowhere.

AmE "attorney" vs BrE "barrister" (if they will be arguing cases in court) or "solicitor" (if they will be doing office-based legal work); "lawyer" is understandable everywhere.

AmE "baggage" vs BrE "luggage". (The literal meaning only; "emotional baggage" is called that everywhere, though it's more likely to be used by an American.)

Bum: in the US, this is a word for someone who is homeless or down on their luck (or sometimes lazy or scruffy), but in Britain it refers to the buttocks. The British usage is starting to spread to the US as of recently.

AmE "elevator" vs BrE "lift" (though "elevator" is now understood, and often used, internationally).

AmE "individual" vs BrE "person" (in phrases like "I saw a suspicious individual/person on the street corner").

AmE "fall" vs BrE "autumn". "Autumn" is also used in the US, but "fall" (in the sense of the season) is not used in BrE anymore.

Fanny: in the US, this means a person's buttocks, but in Britain it means a woman's genital area. Don't have your British characters pat a woman on her fanny unless you're clear on what that means.

AmE "flashlight" vs BrE "torch". My brother-in-law, a New Zealander working in the US in the oil industry at the time, caused consternation among his American colleagues when he was checking inside an empty oil tank and asked someone to hand him a torch, which in the US means welding equipment.

AmE "goosebumps" vs BrE "goose pimples".

Hands up: in Britain, this phrase is used in calling for a vote by show of hands, but in the US it implies raising your hands because you're being threatened by a weapon.

AmE "Holstein" (breed of cow) vs BrE "Ayrshire". (I only include this because I've seen an author use the American word in a Commonwealth English context.)

AmE "janitor" vs BrE "caretaker" (of an institution) or "porter" (of a dwelling).

Knock up: in Britain, this means to wake someone up by knocking on their door. It was a job for a while, in the days after industrialization meant getting up at a specific time was important, but before there were cheap, reliable alarm clocks. In the US, to knock someone up means to get them pregnant, though that usage is now also known worldwide, including Britain. For example, a book by a British author in which the pregnant heroine refers metaphorically to being "knocked down" contains the wry response, "'Down' is not the direction in which you have been knocked."

AmE "mail" vs BrE "post" (specific to Britain). This difference is in how the letters you receive are referred to, and the verb used for sending a letter; both countries talk about a "post office." The mail in America will be brought to you by a mail carrier; the post in Britain will be brought to you by a postman or postie.

AmE "math" vs BrE "maths" (two different ways to abbreviate "mathematics").

AmE "Mom" vs BrE "Mum" as something you call your mother.

AmE "package" vs BrE "packet" (of biscuits or chips, for example) or "parcel" (if it's for sending objects through the post).

AmE "period" (punctuation) vs BrE "full stop".

AmE "raise" vs BrE "rise" (in salary; specific to Britain).

AmE "rowboat" vs BrE "rowing boat".

Rubber: in the US, this is a condom. In Britain, it's what Americans call an eraser, and it's quite innocent for teenagers to carry a rubber in their pencil case.

AmE "sailboat" vs BrE "sailing boat".

AmE "sick" vs BrE "ill". "Unwell" should work anywhere.

AmE "thumbtack" vs BrE "drawing pin".

AmE "vacation" vs BrE "holiday". In AmE, a holiday is a public holiday, what in Britain is often called a "bank holiday". In BrE, it means you are going away for leisure purposes.

Cars (see also On the Street/Going Out)

AME "AUTOMOBILE" VS BrE "car" ("car" is, of course, used in the USA as well).

AmE "body shop" vs BrE "panel beater".

AmE "cab" vs BrE "taxi" ("taxi" is used in both).

AmE "freeway" vs BrE "motorway".

AmE "gas station" vs BrE "petrol station," "filling station" or "service station".

AmE "gearshift" vs BrE "gear lever".

AmE "hood" and "trunk" vs BrE "bonnet" and "boot" (in refence to parts of a car).

AmE "motor" vs BrE "engine" (a "motor" in some parts of Britain, among working-class people at least, is a car; this was a more universal usage in the early 20th century in both Britain and America).

AmE "parking lot" vs BrE "carpark".

AmE "windshield" vs BrE "windscreen".

AmE "wreck" vs BrE "crash" (referring to a car accident).

AmE "wrench" vs BrE "spanner".

Clothing

AME "DERBY" VS BRE "bowler". I read a book not too long ago by an experienced American author, who should have known better, in which one of these hats was repeatedly called a "derby" by his most British character.

Dungarees: in Britain, this means what an American would call bib overalls. In America, it used to mean hard-wearing trousers.

Jumper: in Britain, this is a sweater (that word is also used, along with "pullover" or "jersey"). The garment called a jumper in the US is a pinafore dress in Britain.

Pants: in Britain (not in the Commonwealth) refers specifically to underpants. In the US, and most of the rest of the world, a synonym for trousers.

AmE "sneakers" vs BrE "trainers" (outside Britain, "sneakers" tends to be the term).

AmE "spool of thread" vs BrE "reel of cotton".

Suspenders: in the US, these are what British people call braces, a means of holding up your trousers by looping a strap over the shoulder. In Britain, suspenders hold up stockings; in America, that's a garter belt.

Vest: in Britain (but not in the Commonwealth), this means what is known elsewhere, including the USA, as a singlet or undershirt. In the USA, it means what is known elsewhere, including Britain, as a waistcoat.

AmE "zipper" vs BrE "zip".

Education

AME "ALUMNUS" VS BRE "graduate" if you're talking about a university, or "old boy/girl" if you're talking about a secondary school.

AmE "college" vs BrE "university" (sometimes "varsity" or "uni"; "varsity" is more old-fashioned and pretentious). In British and Commonwealth countries, "college" can sometimes mean a secondary school, though the universities of Oxford and Cambridge (and some other British universities) are made up of a number of colleges as well. Americans are well advised to do some research on terminology and procedures before setting any part of their story in a British university or talking about people who have been to one. For example, an undergraduate degree in Britain and the Commonwealth normally takes three years, not four. The American terminology of "freshman," "sophomore," "junior" and "senior" is not used; the three years are simply first year, second year, third year, if they're called anything, although newly entered scholars are sometimes referred to as "freshers". Up until recently, in fact, British universities generally divided their courses by terms rather than years. The old division of Michaelmas Term (September until Christmas), Hilary Term (January to March) and Trinity Term (mid-April to June) is still used at Oxford; Cambridge calls January to March Lent Term and April to June Easter Term; other British universities and some British schools (and the University of Sydney in Australia until 1989) use similar terminology, but check for the specific place and time you are using as your setting.

AmE "high school" vs BrE "secondary school". ("High school" is used in some parts of the Commonwealth.)

AmE "principal" (of a school) vs BrE "headmaster" or "headmistress". Commonwealth English is slowly adopting the US usage, often alongside the British usage.

Public school: in Britain, confusingly, a "public school" is a private school (the "public" part originally distinguished it from being educated locally or in your own home). What Americans call a public school is a state school in Britain. Check the exact terminology for the period of your setting; it's changed several times over the years.

AmE "recess" vs BrE "break" (meaning a period of time at a school where class is not in session, but it's not lunchtime; in New Zealand when I was at school we called this "interval").

AmE "semester" vs BrE "term". There are typically three terms in an academic year in Britain (see discussion above under college/ university).

Food and Drink

AME "BAR" VS BRE "PUB". There are some technical differences; if you plan to set a scene in one, look them up on Wikipedia.

AmE "can" vs BrE "tin" ("can" is also used; "tin" can also mean a container with a lid, made out of metal, such as you might keep biscuits in).

AmE "candy" vs BrE "sweets".

Chips: in Britain, this means what Americans call French fries (which are actually Belgian, but never mind), as in "fish and chips". What Americans call chips are crisps in the UK, though the American usage is spreading internationally; they were usually called "crisps" when I was a child in New Zealand in the 1970s, but I seldom hear a New Zealander call them anything but "chips" nowadays.

AmE "cookie" vs BrE "biscuit". If you're a baking nerd, there is a technical difference between a cookie and a biscuit (cookies are made from a softer, thicker, denser dough and are generally larger), but as a rule of thumb, call it a biscuit if it's British. What Americans call a biscuit is somewhat, but not exactly, like a British scone.

AmE "cotton candy" vs BrE "candyfloss".

AmE "eggplant" vs BrE "aubergine". Either may be used in BrE outside Britain.

Entree: in the US, this means the main course of a meal, but in BrE it means the appetizer.

Grill: in the US, this means to cook on a barbecue, but in BrE it means what Americans call broiling.

AmE "grilled cheese sandwich" vs BrE "toasted cheese sandwich".

AmE "shrimp" vs BrE "prawn" (though "shrimp" is also understood).

AmE "zucchini" vs BrE "courgette". Either may be used in BrE outside Britain.

Games and Pastimes

AME "CHECKERS" VS BRE "draughts". At the age of about five, I encountered this game under the name of "draughts," but was briefly confused because I'd previously been introduced to it as "checkers" by my American cousins.

AmE "tic-tac-toe" vs BrE "noughts and crosses".

AmE "chutes and ladders" vs BrE "snakes and ladders".

The Home and Family

AME "BABY BUGGY" OR "baby carriage" vs BrE "pram" (originally short for "perambulator").

AmE "bathtub" vs BrE "bath". In Britain and some Commonwealth countries, you are likely to find one of these in a bathroom, and the toilet is often in a separate room; that room is also referred to as the toilet rather than the bathroom. I amused my American wife's sister once when she called to talk to my wife and I said "she's in the toilet," meaning the room rather than the vessel.

AmE "closet" vs BrE "cupboard" or (if it's for clothes) "wardrobe". There's a scene in *Shadowlands*, the play about C.S. Lewis, in which a snarky colleague asks if the American edition of *The Lion, the Witch and the Wardrobe* will be called *The Lion, the Witch and the Clothes Closet*. The BrE term "cupboard" is also used for what in America is called a "cabinet".

AmE "comforter" vs BrE "duvet" or "eiderdown".

AmE "couch" vs BrE "sofa".

AmE "counter" vs BrE "bench" (in the context of a kitchen; a shop counter is still a counter in Britain, presumably because you count out change on it).

AmE "diaper" vs BrE "nappy" (from "napkin").

AmE "drapes" vs BrE "curtains".

AmE "duplex" vs BrE "semi-detached".

AmE "faucet" vs BrE "tap".

AmE "laundry" vs BrE "washing" (referring to the clothes to be washed; "the laundry" in BrE means a place where clothes are washed, not the clothes themselves).

AmE "living room" vs BrE "sitting room," "lounge" or "drawing room" ("living room" is now also used). I have the impression that a sitting room is more downmarket than a drawing room, but do your own research.

AmE "pacifier" vs BrE "dummy" (hence the expression in New Zealand English, "to spit the dummy," meaning to be loudly upset, like a baby who has spat out its dummy and is in full cry).

AmE "pitcher" vs BrE "jug".

AmE "roommate" vs BrE "flatmate". In many cases, people referred to as "roommates" in the US do not actually share a room, but a house or apartment in which they have separate rooms. You can be someone's flatmate in BrE without living in a flat (apartment); if you share a freestanding house, you can still be called flatmates. "Housemate" should be understandable in both dialects.

AmE "stove" vs BrE "cooker" (specific to Britain; other English-speaking countries also say "stove").

AmE "wash up" vs BrE "wash your hands" or "wash the dishes" (the latter can also be "do the washing up," which is specifically British).

AmE "washcloth" vs BrE "flannel".

AmE "yard" vs BrE "garden" (so called even if there are no plants in it). This is specific to the domestic meaning; a prison yard, for example, is still called a yard if you're British.

On the Street/Going Out (see also Cars)

BLOCK: I OCCASIONALLY see books set in Britain with British characters talking about "blocks" (as in "his destination was several blocks away"). Most British cities, being pre-modern, are not laid out on a grid, so British people don't usually measure urban distance in blocks. The BrE equivalent is probably "streets"; "his destination was several streets away," but this doesn't convey an exact distance, since most British urban streets are not standard distances apart.

AmE "druggist" vs BrE "chemist". "Pharmacist" should be understandable internationally, but may not be colloquial for your character.

AmE "hobo" vs BrE "tramp".

AmE "line" vs BrE "queue" (if you're talking about standing in line/queuing for something, such as to be served at a store/shop.)

AmE "movies" vs BrE "cinema," referring to where you go to watch a "movie" (AmE) or "film" (BrE).

AmE "railroad" vs BrE "railway".

AmE "sidewalk" vs BrE "pavement". In New Zealand (possibly elsewhere), we say "footpath." In the US, the "pavement" is the roadway, not the pedestrian area to the side of it.

AmE "store" vs BrE "shop".

AmE "trash" or "garbage" vs BrE "rubbish". Likewise, AmE "trash can" or "garbage can" vs BrE "rubbish bin" or "dustbin" ("dustbin" is specific to Britain).

Is "Alright" All Right?

SPEAKING OF WORD USAGE, is it all right to use "alright"?

tl;dr: No.

But to go into it in more depth: the spelling "alright," last I checked, is still not accepted by major style guides. I see it used often enough that I suspect it's inevitably going to become accepted, taking up a similar position to "altogether" (which means something subtly different from "all together"; "I assembled the suspects all together" versus "there were twelve of them altogether"). But it's not there yet.

It's definitely not a good idea to use it in historical contexts, where it's an anachronism; it's best not to use it at all, in fact, but if you absolutely must, keep it for contemporary. Google Ngram Viewer shows it as unheard-of before about 1900, very rare until the 1960s, and gradually gaining usage until 1995, when it starts to increase in popularity more rapidly. It's still a long way behind "all right"; "all right" was at roughly the same level of popularity in 1860 as "alright" is today, and grew gradually until a peak in about 1945, when it started declining for a while until it swung upwards again around 1980. I'm not sure what replaced it, assuming something did; perhaps things weren't "all right" for a while after World War II.

The replacement wasn't "OK", my first thought, which, though it's existed since at least 1800, only started a significant upswing in 1967 and equaled "all right" in 1980 (both started going up around then, but "OK" went faster). The variant "okay," first seen in the late 1930s, overtook "all right" in 2000 and "OK" in 2005, and is today almost twice as common as "all right", three times as common as "OK", and ten times as common as "alright" in the written corpus Google Ngram Viewer draws on (a large number of scanned books and other written material published between 1800 and 2019).

"All right" wasn't replaced by "fine" either. After some ups and downs in the 19th century, "fine" shows a dip from 1905 to 1918 (understandable), followed by a rise until 1925, then a fairly steady decline from 1925 to 1995, when it starts an upswing more or less parallel to "okay". Of course, "fine" means several other things apart from what "OK" or "all right" mean, even if you restrict your search to the adjective (which you can do in Ngram Viewer by searching for "fine_ADJ").

I checked thesaurus.com for other alternatives and found "very well," which, of course, can also be used in phrases like "she did that very well" (which isn't what we're after, but I'm not sure how you'd eliminate it from the search). "Very well" has been in relatively stable usage since 1800.

If we restrict the usage to the start of the sentence (using the _START_ tag before each word), we get a slightly different picture. This will reduce (though not eliminate) the other usages of "fine" such as "fine furniture" and bring it more into line with the usage of the other words: "All right, let's see what we have here."

Here we see that "fine" at the start of a sentence has a big peak in 1925, after which it slowly declines, crossing "OK" on its way up in 1969. "OK" peaked in 1986 and started declining, with no other words seemingly replacing it. Presumably, people weren't starting their sentences with a filler word meaning "all right" to the same extent.

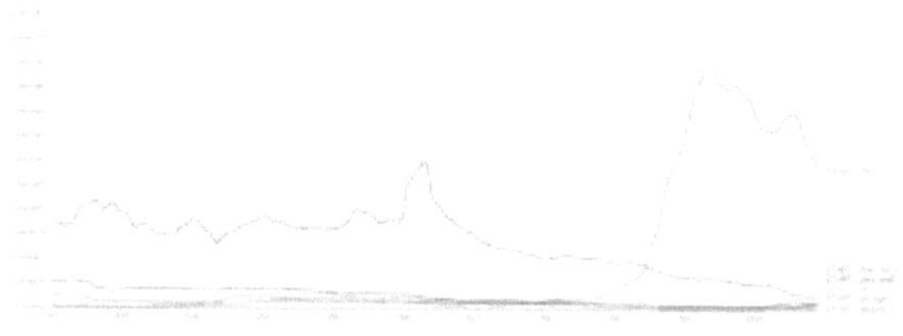

Another way to home in on the usage I'm interested in is to make it part of a phrase, such as "that's okay/OK/fine/all right/alright". (I left out "very well" because "that's very well" is not a phrase people use.) The picture is pretty similar:

So, if your story is set any time between 1800 and about 1980, go with "all right"; it's always correct, and it's something that people of that time period were much more likely to say than most of the alternatives. If they're a more high-flown speaker, "very well" is a good choice in some contexts. "OK" or "okay" are best used after about 1970, though they did exist earlier. But avoid using "alright" except possibly in contemporary or future settings, and even then, I'd advise against it.

X-Year Anniversary

ANOTHER POTENTIAL ANACHRONISM I've come across: "X-year anniversary" (where X is a number). Now, this phrase is strictly redundant, since the "ann" part of "anniversary" comes from the Latin for "year"; I suspect it's become a phrase because people whose relationships don't typically last very long have begun marking "anniversaries" measured in terms of months. But the reason I mention it is not because it's redundant, but because, like "alright," it's a comparatively recent usage (since 1980) and will be anachronistic in any earlier period. It's also still much less often used than "Xth anniversary," which is always safe to use.

Why and How to Research

Of course, you won't do this kind of word research if you don't think about the question of how language has changed in the first place, and this is where the problems start. The past was different. People spoke differently, used different technology, named their children differently, and thought differently about the world. To convey any kind of authentic sense of a past time, you need to be aware that those differences existed, and do the research about what they were.

Reading books and other documents from the time is an excellent way to start to sensitise yourself to possible differences. There are huge digital archives of newspapers and other texts available for free online (maps, too; places change a lot even in a short timespan). Look for specific periodicals (e.g. *The Strand Magazine*, *Harper's*, *Graham's*, *The Century*, *Scribner's*) on Project Gutenberg to get a feel for the time. *The Strand Magazine*, especially, has non-fiction pieces on many institutions in London from 1891 onwards, the period of Sherlock Holmes (whose stories were first published in *The Strand Magazine*). Want a funny story about a cat belonging to the River Police for a bit of colour in your 1890s steampunk mystery? *The Strand Magazine* has you covered. Just the first couple of issues will give you detailed descriptions of the veterinary college, the metropolitan fire brigade, the river police, and the mint, setting out exactly how they worked and some of the notable people involved, and also providing pen-and-ink illustrations.

If you're setting something in a time period, maybe go to a historical library or second-hand bookshop and get some nonfiction works that will tell you what was believed about the world at the time, and some popular fiction that will tell you what people's preoccupations and prejudices were. Your main characters don't need to have the same fears, ambitions, or hatreds as the society in general, but you should be aware of what general attitudes were around. Antisemitism, racism, sexism and a belief in eugenics, the inherent superiority of Europeans over other people, and the excellence of colonialism were widespread a hundred or two hundred years ago, for example, but they were never universal. If you're going for a degree of realism, there probably should be people in your story who hold these attitudes and express them more or less offensively, though of course you're not obliged to include such perspectives at all if that doesn't serve your purpose or if it alienates your audience. But it is not anachronistic to have individuals in your fiction who do not hold these attitudes, who treat people of all kinds of origins as their fellow human beings and their equals. It is anachronistic to imply that people in general didn't hold such attitudes, or to have your characters hold attitudes indistinguishable from those you hold as a 21st-century person, but again, doing so may be more palatable to your audience or more in line with your goals. You should, at least, be aware that you're being anachronistic and have decided consciously that you want to do it anyway.

Many newspapers have online archives, particularly of their older issues. Bear in mind that when newspapers were the only available form of mass media, there were a lot more of them; even a relatively small town would have one, and anywhere of any size would have several competing papers pitched at different demographics and shades of political opinion. Notoriously, newspapers are bad at specific facts, but reading them will give you an idea of the main events, personalities, and controversies of the day, and how a lot of people, guided or misguided by their newspapers, thought about them. The advertisements are also revealing of what was for sale and how it was being sold.

And doing this kind of exercise will develop a critical distance between yourself and your own culture, like an observational comedian who asks, "What's *that* about?" That can only benefit your writing.

Perhaps you aren't concerned with historical accuracy; you just want to put your essentially modern heroine in a corset and crinolines for aesthetic reasons. There will always be plenty of readers who know, and care, less than you do about the period you're setting your story in and just want a fun read that hits their favourite tropes. But I hope that if you're reading a book about how to improve your writing, you might want some advice about improving your research and giving your story at least a veneer of authenticity. It will only ever be a veneer, since you aren't a person from that time, and, since you are writing for contemporary readers, this is a good thing. But a little authentic detail goes a long way in transporting those readers to a different time and place, rather than to a kind of Ren Faire or theme park with a vaguely "history times" aesthetic.

Real Life and Fiction

As I argued above in The Fiction/Fantasy/Worldbuilding Defense, anything you include in your fiction that doesn't have to be fictional should be as realistic as you can reasonably manage.

This includes avoiding the technique that the Turkey City Lexicon (a set of vocabulary for use in critiquing science fiction) refers to as "call a rabbit a smeerp." If something can be the same as it is in real life, and that will work just as well for your story as if it was different in a way that makes no practical difference, then make it the same as real life, and call it the same thing. It gives your reader less to figure out and anchors them to their normal experience amid whatever fictional difference you're presenting, and they will appreciate it.

If your goal is to give your readers the sense of a thoroughly alien world, of course, by all means build in differences that enhance that feeling. In that case, the differences do have a function.

Many people don't have much understanding of how our real world works, though, which is why we sometimes get "worldbuilding" that feels like scenery flats—and scenery flats left over from another production, at that. In this section, you'll find some advice that I hope will help you to improve on that.

First, though, a word about tropes.

Tropes

A **trope** is a common convention of the genre you're writing in. Often, tropes are not closely related to real life. In a cinematic-style thriller, for example, you might have your characters fall from a great height, or be slammed into a wall by an explosion, and then pick themselves up and continue to pursue the villain (instead of sustaining multiple fractures and having to be hospitalised for weeks).

I don't usually count tropes as "getting things wrong," if it's clear from the various genre signals that we're in trope territory. For example, I enjoy the TV show NCIS, even though I know that the speed with which the sole forensic scientist gets her results (and the breadth of her expertise) is completely absurd and driven by plot requirements rather than the realities of actual forensic science. I give it the "trope pass". On the other hand, if you're writing a gritty, realistic police drama, you'll need to put in some research in order to convey that sense of realism.

Some tropes can easily become toxic, too, such as the supposedly intelligent and independent woman who does something stupid and headstrong and has to be rescued by a man; or the stalker or manipulator or abuser as romance "hero"; or the loner drifter who "solves" all his problems with violence and never makes a lasting emotional connection. If you're using a genre trope, give it some thought. Does it line up with your values? Or does it encapsulate values from an earlier era that you don't want to reinforce? How could you undermine it, flip it, subvert it, avert it, give it a nod of acknowledgement without simply following a well-trodden path? Brandon Sanderson is particularly skilled at alluding to a trope without repeating it, and it's part of what makes his fiction great (and popular).

If you have a few hours you don't mind wasting, the website TV Tropes is a vast and amusing collection of tropes with numerous examples, not only from TV (despite the name), but from all fictional media. Use it to familiarise yourself with the tropes of your genre, and as an occasion to reflect on those tropes and what they convey.

As a reader and a reviewer, I also distinguish between, on the one hand, using a trope while being aware that it's not realistic, because the trope is cooler, and on the other hand, being ignorant about how things actually work. If you're writing something I know is a common error, and it doesn't obviously do anything to make your story cooler, I will assume you don't know how it actually works.

Common Errors

RATHER THAN TALK IN depth about research techniques and the best websites to use (which will differ depending on the topic), I want to mention a few things I've seen people get wrong in ways that aren't cooler, just ignorant and incorrect.

Astronomy

A **constellation** is a group of stars that, from Earth (or whatever planet), are in the same part of the sky. They are not necessarily anywhere close to one another in actual space, though; they just happen to be in the same direction from a particular viewpoint. Don't send your space opera heroes to a constellation.

Geosynchronous orbits (where a satellite or similar remains stationary with respect to the surface of the earth) are only possible above the equator, and only at a specific height above the surface, because satellites always orbit the centre of the planet and their speed is related to their altitude. You can't have a geosynchronous orbit positioned above, say, Edinburgh.

There is also a problem specific to fantasy and science-fictional worlds with multiple moons. **The phase of the moon** depends on the relative positions of the moon, the earth, and the sun. This diagram from Wikimedia Commons should make it clear:

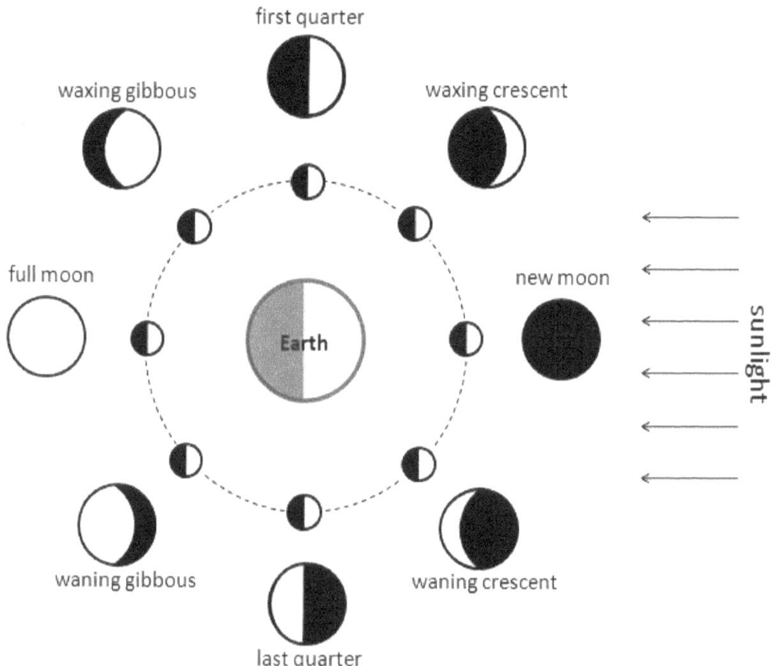

By Andonee - Own work, CC BY-SA 4.0, https://commons.wikimedia.org/w/index.php?curid=38635547

This means that, if you live on a planet with multiple moons, and they are in the same part of the sky, they will have the same phase. They can only be in different phases if they are not close to one another.

Construction

BRICKS ARE NOT STONES, and squared stones are not bricks, they are blocks. Brick-shaped pieces of concrete are not bricks either;

they're also blocks. Bricks are specifically ceramic (made of baked clay).

Cement, technically, is the dry powder; concrete is a mixture of cement, aggregate (sand and small stones), and water.

Embassies

EMBASSIES ARE LOCATED in the capital (or at least the seat of government, which is normally the capital), and deal with government-to-government negotiations, treaties and the like. The equivalent in a non-capital city (such as New York) is called a consulate or consulate general, and the person in charge is a consul or consul general (plural: consuls general). Consulates deal more with administrative matters for citizens of their country in the foreign country where they're located, or for local citizens who want to travel to or do business with their country.

Between countries within the British Commonwealth, the equivalent of an embassy is called a high commission, and the person in charge is a high commissioner.

I've several times seen writers locate embassies in New York, which is incorrect unless, in your fiction, New York is the capital. While permanent representatives to the UN (headquartered in New York) are termed "UN ambassadors" by some countries, and rank equally with ambassadors, their headquarters are not embassies.

Fashion

FASHION HISTORIANS generally roll their eyes at both book covers and screen adaptations of historical fiction, but most of us don't notice. Also, people (especially people who aren't fashionable or can't afford new clothes all the time) do often wear clothes from previous decades, and vintage fashion is now a thing; but if you're writing historical fiction, do attempt some degree of accuracy at least. Historical fashion information, including illustrations, isn't difficult to source. For example, don't give your heroine a reticule (popular about 1795-1820) if your book is set in the 1890s.

Standards of beauty also change over time. One book set in the 1920s gave us "flappers" who were curvy and had long hair, whereas a boyish thinness (achieved in part by smoking) and short hair were two essentials of the flapper look.

Guns

I'M NOT A BIG GUN GUY, but I know the basics, and if you have guns in your story, you should know the basics too.

A revolver and an automatic are different weapons. Don't have one turn into the other over the course of a couple of pages (I've seen this; I've even seen it change back again). In the very early days of the existence of automatic pistols, around the first decade of the 20th century, some writers, who were used to calling pistols "revolvers," incorrectly referred to automatics as revolvers, but they are not.

Revolvers and automatics are both pistols or handguns, but a revolver looks like a Wild West six-shooter, while an automatic is the kind of pistol usually carried by spies and such. When you fire a revolver, the brass cartridges typically stay in the gun, whereas if you fire an automatic they're usually ejected, leading to sounds as they hit the ground, forensic evidence and so forth. As a rule of thumb, a revolver is likely to fire larger bullets. (Incidentally, don't confuse bullets and cartridges either. The bullet is the part that shoots out. The cartridge holds the explosive and stays behind.)

Pistols hold different numbers of shots, depending on the specific model of gun. Pick a model that's appropriate to the place and time of your story—you don't have to mention the name, but you should know it—and read its Wikipedia page. That should tell you how many shots it fires, how much it weighs, how large it is, and other such relevant facts. I read one book in which a character somehow concealed a late-19th-century British service pistol—which would have been a Webley .455, a revolver almost a foot long and weighing about two and a half pounds—under his trouser leg, strapped to his ankle with a necktie.

Again, you don't need to put all your research on the page, but it may suggest things for your story, and at least you won't do something that anyone who knows anything about guns will know is ridiculous.

Any gun will have a calibre, which is the size of ammunition it takes. Make sure you get this right, and punctuate it correctly: it's a .22, for example, but a 9mm, not a ~~.9mm~~.

A rifle and a shotgun are also different weapons. They have different rates of fire, different amounts and kinds of ammunition, are effective at different ranges, and are used to shoot different kinds of game. Deer are hunted with rifles, for example, and birds with shotguns. Again, I've seen more than one author (even one who had been in the army and ought to have known better) change a rifle into a shotgun, and sometimes back again, in the course of a scene. Don't do this.

Finally, there's a difference between an automatic rifle (which can fire multiple shots in a burst if you hold the trigger down) and a semi-automatic rifle (which will, after each shot, prepare the next shot without the user having to work a separate lever, but won't fire again until the trigger is pulled again).

Measurement Systems

DON'T MIX TRADITIONAL measurements like miles, gallons, pounds and acres with metric/SI units like metres, litres, kilograms and hectares, unless your fiction specifically calls for mixing them because of its setting and characters. For example, your story might be set at a time when a country is in transition from one system to the other, or when both are in use for different purposes. I still usually give my height as "six feet" even though I use metric units for everything else in daily life, for example. If you decide to use one or the other, research which would have been in use at the time and place you're setting your story.

If, for some reason, you do use both, make sure you get the conversions correct. I read a book in which a character estimated a distance as "maybe a thousand metres. Less than half a mile," but since a mile is roughly 1600 meters, a thousand meters is in fact about ⅝ of a mile, which is more than half. In general, I find the use of metric units in medieval-style fantasy novels (such as the one I just quoted) anachronistic, given that the metric system came out of the French Revolution, though you should consider your intended audience and what measurements they will be familiar with. Fantasy novels set in another world do get an implicit "pseudotranslation" pass; since they're in a world with a history and language different to ours, you can claim that some of the cultural features and even names have been silently translated to preserve understanding for the reader. Samwise Gamgee, according to Tolkien, was actually named Banazîr Galbasi, but "Samwise Gamgee" gives the equivalent feel to an English-speaking reader that the "original" name had in the Westron language. So you can pretend that your medievalesque fantasy characters are using meters and centimeters for measurement if it makes your readers' lives easier. Try not to push the pseudotranslation defense too hard, though.

I've several times seen stories set in England prior to the 1970s use metric measurements instead of Imperial (traditional) measurements for things like land area. Britain did not officially adopt the metric system until 1969, and imperial measurements are still in use in several everyday contexts in Britain, sometimes alongside metric measures. Metrication is still not complete or legally required in all contexts, either. However, British scientists have used the metric system since the mid-19th century.

Note also that some British Imperial measurements that have the same name as American traditional measurements are not the same size (gallons, for example).

A **league** is an old-fashioned measure of distance defined roughly as the distance a person can walk in an hour, which for the average person is about three miles. Of course, before accurate clocks, the concept of an hour was fairly flexible, and in some cases changed with the seasons so that there were an even number of hours in the daytime and the nighttime, so occasionally an hour was (circularly) defined as the time it took to walk a league.

In any case, be aware that a league is roughly three miles and takes approximately an hour to walk at an average pace. I've seen "leagues" that are a lot shorter than that.

Patents

PATENTS ARE PUBLIC. You can't have a "secret patent". The word itself means "lay open" or "make available for public inspection". The secret alternative is a "trade secret". Unlike a patent, which has an expiry date, a trade secret can continue to be used for profit as long as the holder is able to protect the secret, which they can do through non-disclosure agreements, the restriction of the secret to a small number of people, and special procedures for handling and storing such things as formulas or designs. If the holder of a trade secret takes reasonable steps to protect it, another company that obtains it by methods such as industrial espionage breaks the law and can be prosecuted. Like everything to do with the law, the details differ at different times and in different places; do your research.

Zoology

IT'S A COMMON MISCONCEPTION (no doubt fed by art aimed at children) that polar bears and penguins are found living side by side. Polar bears live in the Arctic (the north), and penguins live in the Antarctic (the south), and never the twain shall meet, at least not outside a zoo. Seals, however, live in both the Arctic and Antarctic.

Weasels, ferrets, and stoats are not rodents (though squirrels are).

Rabbits are not rodents either, though they were classified as such until the early 20th century, and they are also not hares, or vice versa; rabbits and hares are different species with a similar body plan.

Most people know this, but a mule is not a donkey; it's the offspring of a donkey and a horse. And while a pony is a horse, a horse is not necessarily a pony; a pony is specifically a small breed of horse. Likewise, a mustang is a horse, but it's a specific kind of horse, namely a feral (wild) horse; don't have mustangs pulling carts in your book.

The broader principle is: Before you use what you think is a synonym, check that it actually is.

Horses are often treated in historical and fantasy fiction as if they're mechanical vehicles that can travel long distances rapidly without food, water, or rest. This is, of course, not the case. It could be considered a genre trope, and if you want to ignore realism, you can do that, but here are some realities of travel by horse.

An average horse can walk about as fast, and about as far, as a reasonably fit human: 3-4 miles an hour (5 to 6.5 km/h) and about 20-30 miles a day (30-50 km). A very fit, endurance-trained horse or one bred to do so can travel up to 50 miles (80 km) in a day, while one who is old or in poor condition may only get about 15 miles (24 km).

That's assuming that the horse is travelling at a walk. They can go faster at a trot (10 mph or 16 km/h), canter (15 mph or 24 km/h) or gallop (20 or more mph, 35 or more km/h), but they can't sustain those paces for as long as a walk. You will trade off speed for distance and probably not be able to go much further, if at all, at least if you are talking about a day of travel. Also, you risk harming your horse if you keep them at a fast speed. Stories in which people gallop their horses for days at a stretch without rest are not remotely realistic, either in terms of what horses can do or what people can do, but of course you can argue that in a fantasy world, heroes (and their horses) have special abilities. Tolkien, who grew up in an England where horses were used as everyday transport, would have known that the feats of endurance and speed he attributed to Gandalf's horse Shadowfax were unrealistic, just as the endurance run by Gimli, Legolas and Aragorn across Rohan is unrealistic, but they are specifically presented as not being like ordinary humans, or, in Shadowfax's case, ordinary horses.

Historically, people who wanted to travel long distances fast on horseback would periodically change horses, either at prearranged locations where fresh horses were kept, as in the Pony Express (which had stations about 10 or 15 miles apart), or by travelling with more than one horse and switching out which one they were riding, since carrying a rider requires more effort from the horse.

That raises another point: the more weight a horse is carrying—rider and gear—the more energy it requires. This is why Pony Express riders, jockeys, and other post riders had to be small. An armoured knight in full gear, who is probably a large person already, is going to need a big horse, and that horse will need a lot of food, probably including oats or similar high-calorie feed—not just the odd bit of grass cropped from the side of the road while the knight is briefly resting. If you carry these provisions on the horse, that increases the weight further, which is why, unless he's impoverished, a knight should probably have a pack horse or mule as well for a long journey. Likewise, if your Fated Couple have to share a horse for plot reasons, that will reduce the horse's speed and range.

The main advantage of riding a horse is not speed or distance, but the ability to move yourself and your gear with less effort (less effort from you, that is; the horse is putting in a lot of the work). It's still tiring to ride for a long period, especially if you're not used to it. This is something that most writers do seem to know.

Blocking

B locking is the theatre term for figuring out how the actors will move around the stage. In relation to written fiction, it has a similar meaning: figuring out how your characters will move within the scene.

That doesn't just mean where they will walk and where they will stand, but which direction they're facing, what they can therefore see, and what they have in their hands. I read one book (traditionally published) in which the main character spent part of the time walking with a stick following an injury, but was still able to carry two milkshakes. That wasn't the only time she apparently had three hands in the book, either.

That author needed to work on his blocking. So did the other trad-pub author duo who had a character hit another character in the elbow with a tray while they were facing each other. It is possible, but only if one character is standing there with their hands on their head in the middle of a fight. (And how the same authors thought that you could punch someone in the kidneys when they're facing you remains a mystery to me.)

I've also seen this, which again suggests the character had three hands:

> ~~...put her hands on his shoulders, took one finger under his chin, and lifted it...~~

The way I approach blocking is to draw diagrams. They don't have to be elaborate or to scale. A pencil-and-paper sketch is fine for my purposes. If you have action figures, D&D minis or LEGO minifigs, even better—you can set them up in 3D and take pictures from various angles. In real-life locations (for my urban fantasy series, Auckland Allies) I've taken photos or video.

Not only does this avoid describing the impossible, it can open your eyes to new possibilities. When I scout a real location with my GoPro camera strapped to my head (people look at you strangely, but nobody's ever said anything; your culture's concept of politeness may vary), I often come up with new bits of action that are better than what I had in mind. The details of the real, concrete location stimulate thoughts that are an improvement on my vague imaginings.

For example, I'd written a chase scene through an indoor urban environment, a public space with shops on multiple levels, but hadn't visited it. When I did visit it, I realised that someone being pursued through it would have to run from one side of the central atrium to the other to descend the next escalator, that the escalators were narrow enough that if a couple of people were side by side ahead of the person fleeing, that person wouldn't be able to get past them, and that the pursuer would be able to see the fugitive across the three-storey central space, all of which helped to bump up the challenge and tension of the scene.

I don't suggest you do a diagram for every scene. If your characters are sitting talking in a café, it doesn't matter how it's laid out or where they're seated—unless they're going to have to flee out the back when the antagonist attacks, or notice something happening across the street. But if you're writing a major action set-piece, it helps to have an idea of the location, real or fictional: the entrances, exits, items behind which people could hide or shelter, and so forth. Classic murder mysteries often included hand-drawn diagrams of the room where the body was found or the house as a whole, which may be over the top to include in your book, but consider it if doing so would make it easier to describe things in an easy-to-understand way.

Continuity

Besides blocking, there's **continuity**. Blocking will tell you that someone walking with a cane doesn't have two hands free to carry two milkshakes. Continuity tells you that the character has got into a stationary car earlier in the scene and can't, therefore, get into it again without first getting out (same book as the cane and the milkshakes), or that if the character started out on the seventh floor and goes up two storeys they won't reach the eleventh floor (still the same book). The same author in a different book commits a massive continuity error: there are two copies of a significant object, and the narrative is not consistent as to which of them was used for what or where they each ended up, and never explains why the original owner of whichever one it was that did the second thing doesn't appear to have it now, since they would use it again if they had it. It was such a blatant error that I was far from the only reviewer who noticed it. (Apologies for the vagueness, but I'm trying not to make the author too easy to identify.)

Another book by a different author gives us a west gate that has, a couple of chapters later, become the east gate, and a period of "more than a year, but less than two" that a few pages later is more than a *month*, but less than two.

Keeping things consistent is hard, especially if you change your mind a lot. I used to plan my books less carefully than I do now, which meant a lot of revision, and on at least one occasion my editor has picked up that I had a character in a scene that I'd previously cut out of the novel. It's a lot easier in short stories, of course, where you don't have as much to keep track of and the beginning and end are much closer together.

For world-level continuity, I recommend using a wiki (similar to Wikipedia, but there are plenty of lightweight alternatives). It enables you to make entries for people, places, things, institutions, ideas and the like and create hyperlinks between them. Any world in which you set more than a couple of stories will be a lot easier to keep consistent if you take the time to create one of these and keep it up to date.

If a wiki seems like overkill, you can keep a document, or even a spreadsheet, to keep track of characters and important places and things. If you mention a character's eye colour, for example, write it on the document or spreadsheet to make sure that it stays the same. (And by the way, can we stop with the YA protagonists or love interests that all have green eyes? As a green-eyed person myself, I roll those green eyes every time this tired cliché shows itself. I even read a YA short story in which the protagonist was of Indian and Asian descent, but, presumably because she was the protagonist, still somehow had green eyes.)

Also record other physical details that are mentioned, like whether a character is left-handed, or what perfume someone wears, or a distinctive item of clothing or possession. Record the character's name when they're introduced, and make sure you keep spelling it the same way (you would not believe how often I see character names change spelling in the course of a book).

For places and things, as much as for characters, it can help to write down a note when they're first introduced and keep the notes updated as you revise. Just like people, places need to have consistent names and descriptions (and shapes, unless you're writing fantastical stories in which they morph and change—this is where maps and diagrams become useful). Items that go in and out of a character's possession are important to track, too. You don't need to mention all the time where they are—I read a very tedious novel by a major writer which kept telling me exactly where the protagonist put her bag, even though it never mattered even once—but keep track of whether an object has been lost or used up so that you don't bring it back in a later scene and cause a continuity error.

If you find that your documents are growing out of control, consider the wiki solution. It's really no harder.

Some editors work specifically on continuity. They will pick up that the character you called Tom on page 60 is Don on page 65, or that the fight announcer said they were going to start with four people fighting and then the fight only involved two people, or that the gun that's used in book fourteen was lost overboard at the end of book twelve (all real examples, the last one from a New York Times bestselling author). Some of the advice in this chapter comes from one such continuity editor, Adriel Wiggins (http://mrsawiggins05.wordpress.com/), and I'm grateful for her assistance.

Timelines

I generally do a timeline of my books fairly late in the revision process, if the events are complex enough to need a timeline at all, but you could do one at any point, including when you're planning the story outline. This helps to make sure that you don't have two Fridays in the same week, and that there's room for everything to happen—without big gaps in which nothing happens and there's nothing to account for why the characters were sitting on their hands. In a book with a "ticking clock" that you use to provide tension, a timeline is especially important.

Sometimes, I find that I've messed up the timeline and have to revise to make it consistent. I'm not alone in this. Tolkien mentions somewhere that when he was revising *The Lord of the Rings* he had to do a rewrite because he had the moon in different phases on the same day in two different places.

Moon phases are important if you mention the moon more than once (and, obviously, if you're writing a werewolf book), just as tides are important if your setting includes a coast, and the season is important if there's weather.

There's a software tool called AeonTimeline which can help you with a complex fictional timeline, even if your world has a calendar that is not our familiar calendar. It integrates with Scrivener, the popular writing software. When I trialled it a while ago it seemed tedious to move large numbers of items around, but I understand it may have improved since. You can get a free trial version at http://www.scribblecode.com/. Another product called World Anvil (http://worldanvil.com), created for roleplaying games, also enables you to integrate timelines, maps, characters and even objects, and includes novel writing features; it would be a potential alternative to the wiki suggested above. Both of these are paid-for commercial software (which will be tax deductible if you make income from your writing, in most countries), though WorldAnvil has a free tier with a number of basic features. I am not an affiliate for either of these products; I'm just pointing you to them because you might find them useful.

Section 2: Grammatical Building Blocks

By necessity, I've had to use a lot of grammatical terminology in this book so far. This section is in case you're rusty on that terminology, or have never been taught it. Most of it is not things that a lot of people get wrong, which is why it's in this section instead of the main part of the book.

You may have been bored and confused in the past by someone trying to teach you the basic mechanics of language. I'll do my best to make them interesting and clear for you.

Then again, practicing scales and chords can be dull too. And as scales and chords are to music, so the basics of grammar, sentence structure and punctuation are to writing. I won't insist that you have to understand them in order to write well—a lot of great authors write "by ear"—but it's going to make it a lot easier to understand and work on the weaknesses in your writing if you have some terminology and know how the parts fit together. To change the metaphor, if you want to strengthen your body, knowing a little bit of basic anatomy is going to help you to choose the right exercises. If you want to strengthen your writing, the same thing applies.

It's also a lot easier to judge where to put, for example, a comma if you understand how words group together in a sentence and where the boundaries of those groups occur. A lot of the comma errors I see in published books are there because the author didn't realise they were putting a comma in the middle of something, instead of at the boundary.

I use grammatical terms throughout this book. I use these terms for two reasons: firstly, so I don't have to describe what I mean each time, and secondly, because if you're curious about something and want to learn more about it, the correct term helps you to look for more resources.

You don't need to memorise the terminology. There won't be a test on it. It's only there to help you learn the more important practical skills, and you can forget it as soon as you've done so.

Accordingly, we'll go through nouns, pronouns, adjectives, adverbs, verbs, prepositions, conjunctions and sentence structure—but not just for the sake of the theory. Remember, the goal is that you know *just enough to look professional*, so our focus will always be on relating the grammar to strengthening your writing and eliminating common errors.

Subject, Verb and Object

The very basic, high-level structure of a sentence is subject, verb and (optionally) object. That is, someone or something does something, often to someone or something else. (This is also a basic unit of story.)

So, to use an example beloved of my favourite teacher:

> The alligator ate the aardvark.

Here, *the alligator* is the subject. It's doing the action. The action—the verb—is *ate*. And the unfortunate object is *the aardvark*, which is said, appropriately in this case, to be "suffering the action of the verb".

Not every sentence needs an object, depending on the verb. You can just say:

> The alligator ate.

Some verbs require an object, some do not permit an object, and some (like *ate*) can go either way. Most native speakers know which category a verb falls into without thinking about it, and I seldom see people getting this wrong, so I won't spend more time on it here. I do give a couple of examples in the vocabulary chapter, though.

The subject, and the object if there is one, will each be one of three things:

1. A **noun**—the name of a person, place or thing, sometimes accompanied by *the*, *a* or *an* (which are known as

“articles”).

2. A **pronoun**—one of a limited list of words which can stand in for a noun, like *he*, *she* or *it*. (There are other pronouns too, which I'll talk about below.)
3. A **noun phrase**—a group of words which, grammatically, acts like a noun, even though it has internal structure, and not all of its parts are necessarily nouns themselves.

Let's look at nouns and noun phrases in more depth, before we move on to pronouns.

Nouns and Noun Phrases

N*ouns* name people (John, the Pope, Queen Elizabeth, my brother), places (my bedside drawer, Michigan, Lake Geneva, Mount Everest, the Pacific Ocean, the Czech Republic, the corner of Fifth and Broadway), or things, physical or otherwise (lint, iron ore, General Motors, a pebble, an inchoate longing for completion, the Doctrine of Signatures). For capitalisation rules, see that section.

As you've already seen from my examples, nouns aren't always single words. A *noun phrase* is a group of words that can stand in place of a noun, and can be considered a single unit for purposes of grammar (and punctuation).

Not every word in a noun phrase needs to be a noun. For example, you can have a noun phrase that's largely made up of adjectives:

A wide green ocean.

Compound Nouns

COMPOUND NOUNS ARE made up of two or more words that are thought of as a single unit, but haven't quite fused into a single word. The formal term for fusing into a single word is being "styled closed," while two separate words with a space between them are "styled open". The third option is for the two words to be joined by a hyphen.

It's always a good idea to check in whatever dictionary or style guide you use as your reference what the styling is for a particular compound noun. This is because *there aren't any specific rules*. You just have to make a call and then be consistent (and always looking it up in the same dictionary or style guide will ensure you're consistent). For example, "ink well," "inkwell" and "ink-well" are all valid. Not all three forms are always valid, though, which is why you need to check.

Adjectives and Adverbs

Adjectives describe nouns, while adverbs describe verbs (which is why they have the word "verb" in their name).

You'll read advice in some places to minimise your use of adjectives and adverbs, and instead choose more specific and powerful nouns and verbs: "ebony" rather than "black wood" and "she crept" rather than "she walked slowly". In general, that's good advice, but bear in mind how your characters would talk.

Adjectives

AN ADJECTIVE IS A WORD (or phrase, as we'll see) that describes a noun:

A white house.

"White" is the adjective in that sentence. We could also have said large, gloomy, abandoned, palatial or any of a number of other words that describe a house.

Adjectives usually answer the questions: *which, what kind of, how many*?

Which boys? The *orphan* boys.

What kind of house? A *palatial* house.

How many aardvarks? *Two* aardvarks.

(Yes, numbers count as adjectives in this case.)

Adjectival Phrases

AN ADJECTIVAL PHRASE is a group of words that, taken together, modify a noun. Not all of the words in an adjectival phrase need to be adjectives. In fact, it's possible for none of the individual words to be an adjective.

This is a once-in-a-lifetime opportunity.

"Once in a lifetime" is a description of the kind of opportunity it was. But "once" is an adverb (it usually describes how, or rather how often, something is done); "in" is a preposition; "a" is an article; and "lifetime" is a noun. Nevertheless, because the whole phrase modifies a noun, it is an adjectival phrase.

Adjectival phrases are often hyphenated, as in the example. See Hyphenation for more information.

Adverbs

A dverbs describe verbs. They tell us *how* someone or something did an action:

Henrietta **slowly** drew her weapon.

The basic sentence here is subject-verb-object:

Henrietta [subject] drew [verb] her weapon [object].

"Slowly" modifies the verb.

As with adjectives, but even more often, you'll see people advising you to minimise your adverbs and use more precise verbs instead. You still need to know how adverbs work for the occasions when you do use them.

Not all adverbs end in -ly, and not everything that ends in -ly is an adverb. *Lonely*, for example, is an adjective, despite the -ly ending. *More* is an adverb, and there's no such word as ~~morely~~. Some adverbs can use the same form as the corresponding adjectives, like *fast, hard, close* or *deep*, though the forms *hardly, closely* and *deeply* also exist (sometimes with subtly different usages or meanings: *hold me close{ly}* but *stand close to me*; *I hit him hard* versus *I hardly hit him*).

Just as you can have noun phrases and adjectival phrases, you can have adverbial phrases:

Henrietta drew her weapon **with a rakish gesture.**

"With a rakish gesture" answers the question "how did Henrietta draw her weapon?" That makes it an adverbial phrase, even though no individual word in it is an adverb. Notice, too, that the phrase doesn't have to appear next to the verb in order to modify it. And unlike the hyphens for adjectival phrases, there is no special punctuation to signal adverbial phrases.

Adverbial phrases often become sentence modifiers. There is a pitfall to them, discussed under Dangling Modifiers.

Verbs

Verbs, the meat in the subject-verb-object sandwich, tell us what the subject does (to the object, if there is one). The most important thing about verbs is that they have *tense* and *aspect*.

Tense and Aspect

TENSE SIGNALS THE *location* of events in time (past, present, future), while aspect signals their *shape* in time (one-time, continuous, repeated).

Let's look at tense first. Here are the tenses available to you in English:

- Future: *I will eat.* (In British English, especially older or more high-status versions: *I shall eat.*)

- Present: *I am eating* or *I eat.*

- Present perfect: *I have eaten.* (As at the present moment, my eating took place in the past, and is complete.)

- Simple past: *I ate.*

- Past perfect: *I had eaten.* (That is, at a defined point in the past, this action was already completed.)

Now, aspect:

- *I eat* (it's my habit to eat, I do it repeatedly).

- *I am eating* (I'm doing it right now and it's a continuous action).

- *I was eating* (I'm not doing it any longer, but when I did it was an action that extended for a period of time).

As you can see, tense and aspect can't be completely separated.

English has both regular and irregular verbs. The definitional distinction between the two is that regular verbs use the same form in both simple past and past participle (the form used in the present perfect and past perfect), and that form ends in -ed:

I jump, I have jumped, I jumped, I had jumped.

Irregular verbs don't follow this pattern. For example:

I eat, I have eaten, I ate, I had eaten.

In the irregular verb "to eat," the simple past is not formed with -ed, but with a change of vowel. The past participle is also not the same as the simple past.

There are at least a couple of hundred irregular verbs in English, and they include many of the most commonly used verbs. This isn't unusual for a language. Often, the words that get used all the time retain older forms for longer after a major grammatical shift, and also the core vocabulary of English comes from its Germanic roots, where verbs often changed their vowels to signal changes in tense, while a lot of other vocabulary was "borrowed" from other languages after the shift had already taken place and then conformed to the more consistent "regular" pattern.

The most important regular verbs to be aware of are these, because they are even more irregular than most:

I am, he/she/it is, they/you are; I/he/she/it was, they/you were; I/she/they/you had been.

I go, I went, I had gone.

I do, I did, I had done.

Some verbs that used to be irregular, but aren't used very often, like *chide*, eventually start conforming to the regular pattern, so the past tense is no longer *chid* but *chided*. Some verbs are currently partway through this transition, so you can say either *shined* or *shone*, for example. British English tends to favour "shone" except in the specialized sense of "polished" ("he shined his shoes"). In cases like these, if both seem equally correct to you, you should pick one option and stick with it; I have seen an author use both *shined* and *shone* in consecutive sentences with no difference in meaning, which isn't good practice.

My personal observation is that Americans are more likely to use the regular form and British people the irregular form, but I don't have a proper study to back that up. Perhaps I'm mainly thinking of the -t versus -ed ending, such as in *spelt* and *spelled*, *dreamt* and *dreamed*, *leapt* and *leaped*, *burnt* and *burned*, *learnt* and *learned*, *leant* and *leaned*, *smelt* and *smelled*, *spoilt* and *spoiled* and a few others, where the -t ending is used in British English and the -ed ending in US English (generally).

There are also dialects that retain, or possibly even introduce, irregular forms where the more standard language has regular ones, such as *dove* instead of *dived* as the past tense of *dive*. That one is more common in the US, a counter-example to my suggestion above that the US tends to use the regular form in preference to the irregular. So is "drug" as the past tense of "drag," a (minority) US usage; the more common past tense of "drag" is "dragged".

Southern US colloquial English frequently uses the simple past instead of the past participle, too, saying, for example, "I should have went" instead of "I should have gone". Occasionally, it also uses the same form for simple past as for present, as in the case of *spit*, where the simple past in standard English is *spat*.

See my discussion of lay versus lie for a perspective on how you should approach writing narrative and dialog for characters who are not supposed to be speaking in your dialect.

See also the Wikipedia article on English irregular verbs[1], which I drew upon for this section.

Using "Active" Verbs

HERE'S A PIECE OF ADVICE that used to confuse and frustrate me. I would see someone saying, "Don't write passive sentences that use the verb 'to be'," and I would respond, "Using the verb 'to be' doesn't make it passive!"

I was confused because there are two things, both called "passive," which involve the verb "to be". Let me see if I can unconfuse them for you.

The Passive Voice

THE ONE YOU'RE MOST likely to have heard of is the "passive voice". That's when you get a sentence like this:

Mistakes were made.

Or one like this:

John was hit in the head by Fred.

---

1. https://en.wikipedia.org/wiki/English_irregular_verbs

They're "passive voice" because the subject of the sentence is either missing (as in the first example) or taken out of its usual focal position (as in the second example). The "active voice" is the more usual one:

Bureaucrats made mistakes.

Fred hit John in the head.

There's a famous test for passive voice: if you can add the words "by zombies" to the end of the sentence (or if it has an equivalent set of words there already), and it still makes sense, then you have passive voice.

Mistakes were made by zombies.

(I don't know why it should be zombies. Why not aardvarks?)

There's something else to remember about the passive voice. Like the past perfect and present perfect tenses, it uses the *past participle*, not the simple past. For most English verbs, this is a distinction that makes no difference, because the two are the same, but for irregular verbs, they are not.

The alligator *ate* the aardvark.

The aardvark *was eaten*.

Passive voice has its place, but its place is usually in dialog where you want to point up the fact that someone is avoiding responsibility or trying to downplay their role in a problem. Otherwise, active voice is usually the way to go.

Passive Sentences

THE SECOND USE OF "PASSIVE" versus "active" goes like this.

A "passive sentence" is one where the subject is just sitting there, being whatever it is.

The wall was painted white.

It's a perfectly valid sentence, but it's dull. The subject isn't taking action. Compare:

The wall gleamed with white paint.

Now the wall is a bit more exciting. It's doing, rather than just being.

You know who writes a lot of passive sentences, though? Neil Gaiman. One of the few living writers who's both a commercial and critical success, a man who must just about need an extra house by now just in order to store his awards, and what's more, can afford one.

On the other hand, you know who isn't Neil Gaiman? You. (Which isn't entirely a bad thing, according to recent allegations, but anyway...)

Since you probably don't have Gaiman's mastery of mythic storytelling, you need to find any advantage you can, and making your sentences active is an easy way to perk up your prose.

Prepositions

A preposition is a word that tells you the relationship in space or time between two things, like *out, from, in, of, under, between, into, after*.

There's an increasingly common error with *between*, where it's used with only one object. See the Clarity of Reference section under Between.

Some prescriptive grammarians say that the following (known as "preposition stranding") is incorrect:

Who did you go with?

They prefer "preposition fronting":

With whom did you go?

This is not an actual rule of English. The first usage is much more common than the second in actual English speech and writing, and the second is excessively formal. Of course, if your character is excessively formal, this may be just the way to show it.

Prepositions in Idioms

PREPOSITIONS ARE OFTEN used metaphorically, and there are hundreds or even thousands of idioms in English that use prepositions, like "get it off my chest" and "say it to his face". Non-native speakers, and even some native speakers, sometimes have trouble remembering which preposition goes in which phrase.

There's no simple shortcut, because the choice of prepositions for an idiom usually doesn't follow any rules or logic, just tradition.

Check a dictionary if you are at all unsure. The entry for the main word should give common idioms that use that word, and their meaning. If you know you're not good at these, get someone who is good at them to check your work before publishing.

Other Resources

Rather than give you a long list of mediocre resources, I want to give you a few really good ones in each category.

Websites

Grammar Girl (Mignon Fogarty) explains grammar clearly and well (she also has a podcast): http://www.quickanddirtytips.com/grammar-girl

Karen Conlin and Ray Vallese offer tips on usage, mechanics and grammar for working writers at Grammargeddon: http://grammargeddon.com/

Podcasts

Mignon Fogarty's podcast can be found from her website (http://www.quickanddirtytips.com/grammar-girl).

Writing Excuses (http://www.writingexcuses.com) is an excellent podcast by four working writers, full of practical material on how to write. Its focus isn't on what this book is about, but on the business of writing and the storytelling aspect. It's mainly focussed on speculative fiction, since that's what the podcasters write, but they do talk about other genres and about skills that apply to all fiction writing.

The Odyssey Podcast (http://www.sff.net/odyssey/podcasts.html) consists of extracts from the annual Odyssey Writing Workshops, by speculative fiction writers and editors. It's well worth listening to if you're an intermediate writer looking for your next step.

Video

Brandon Sanderson, one of the writers involved in the Writing Excuses podcast, also teaches a course on writing at Brigham Young University, and video recordings of many of his lectures are available on YouTube.

Craft Books

These books also aren't about the language skills I've been talking about in this book, but about the storytelling skills that you also need to be a successful writer.

There are a great many basic books; a good one is *Writing Fiction*, ed. Alexander Steele (from the Gotham Writers' Workshop; pub. A&C Black, 2003).

For the intermediate writer who's read some basic advice, and wants to write stories that will really attract the attention of editors because they stand out from the usual run, I recommend *Wonderbook: The Illustrated Guide to Creating Imaginative Fiction*, by Jeff Vandermeer (pub. Abrams Image, 2013). The related website, http://www.wonderbooknow.com, has even more resources.

Creating Short Fiction by Damon Knight (pub. St. Martin's Griffin, 1985) combines excellent general advice on writing with some specifics on short-story writing that I haven't seen elsewhere. The author was a skilled writer himself, and also lectured at the famous Clarion Writers' Workshop for almost 30 years. Parts of it are, of course, dated (the part about how submissions work, in particular), but most of it still stands up.

Award-winning author Nancy Kress has a couple of fine craft books; I especially recommend *Beginnings, Middles and Ends* (pub. Writer's Digest, 1999), but *Characters, Emotion & Viewpoint: Techniques and Exercises for Crafting Dynamic Characters and Effective Viewpoints* (pub. Writer's Digest, 2005) is also very good.

Finally, if you want to write exciting, action-packed books that flow logically through a plot that makes sense, while also providing some space for reflection and characterisation, you can't do better than the classic *Scene & Structure*, by Jack M. Bickham (pub. Writer's Digest, 1999).

Fiction

If you want to learn to write good fiction, you need to read good fiction. Consider reading some classics, for example. Make sure you're getting a good, clean edition, not some cheaply scanned rubbish full of character recognition errors that hasn't been spellchecked. The editions from Project Gutenberg, especially the major books that have been out for a while, are generally good, while editions from Open Road are often, though not always, poorly proofread; they're a business with only a limited amount of money to devote to proofreading, presumably, while Project Gutenberg uses volunteers and therefore quite likely has a lot more time dedicated to each book. Be aware, with older classics, that punctuation conventions have changed over the years; Dickens, for example, often places a comma before the main verb when he's started a sentence with a long, complicated noun phrase, which today is technically incorrect. And if you read Mary Wollstonecraft's *A Vindication of the Rights of Women*, from a slightly earlier time than Dickens, you will come away with two strong impressions: she really hated the patriarchy, and she really loved commas.

English-language classics that are widely regarded as both expertly written and relatively accessible to modern readers include Dickens' better-known novels (*Great Expectations, Oliver Twist, A Tale of Two Cities, Bleak House, David Copperfield*); Jane Austen's *Pride and Prejudice, Emma,* and *Sense and Sensibility*; George Eliot's *Middlemarch*; and Samuel Richardson's *Joseph Andrews* and *Tom Jones.* Most of these have a humour element in them somewhere, sometimes a strong one; comic novels are hard to do and also fun, and you can learn a lot from reading them. Many of the early books by that great master of the English language, P.G. Wodehouse, are now out of copyright and available on Project Gutenberg. Be aware that he's given to using coincidence to bring his cast together, which I don't recommend imitating.

The craft of writing has, of course, moved on from these books, however excellently they are written, and you also need to be aware of good writing being produced today. Read those writers in your genre who write especially well, too. In my genre, fantasy and science fiction, that would include: Elizabeth Bear, Octavia Butler, Susanna Clarke, Neil Gaiman, Rachel Hartman, Ursula K. Le Guin, Ann Leckie, Scott Lynch, Patricia A. McKillip, Robin McKinley and Naomi Novik. Not only do they tell a good story, but they tell it with mastery of language. Brandon Sanderson, though he doesn't use language to quite the level that those writers do, has a solid grasp of his craft, and his books are excellently edited. The same can be said of Marie Brennan, Genevieve Cogman, and the indie author Melissa McShane. Sanderson is also remarkable for his high-concept worldbuilding, and for linking his worldbuilding into his plot so that the story he's telling couldn't happen in any other world.

It's also worth reading capable authors who are not in the genre you write in. Genre can too easily become a silo, in which people reproduce the same tropes and the same approaches to storytelling. Reading outside your genre can spark new ideas. Also, even if you don't primarily write mystery or romance, those are the two plots that most Western readers know the best, and if you need a subplot, a mystery or a romance is a great candidate—so reading good mysteries and good romances may be beneficial.

Why read these authors? Let me tell you my favourite teaching story, "Beginning to Teach About Jade".

There was once a young Chinese boy who was lucky enough to be given an apprenticeship to a famous jade master. On the first day of his apprenticeship, he hurried to the master's house, eager for the old man to begin to teach him about jade.

When he arrived, though, the master gave him a pebble of jade to hold, and talked to him about his family and the schooling he had had so far, every topic imaginable—except jade. The boy was disappointed, but as he walked home he thought, "The master was just getting to know me. Tomorrow, he will begin to teach about jade."

Next day, though, the master again put a pebble of jade in the boy's hand and began to talk to him about all the Ten Thousand Things—except jade.

Day after day, it was the same. The boy trudged to the master's house, the old man put a pebble of jade in his hand, and he talked about everything under the sun—except jade.

The boy began to despair. "Have I failed some test?" he thought. "Does the master think I am not worthy? Will he never begin to teach about jade?"

He had been raised to be polite and not question his elders, but one day it was too much for him. As he dragged his feet to the master's house, he decided to say something, to ask the master when he would begin to teach about jade.

But on this day, when the master, as was his custom, put the pebble into his hand, the apprentice cried out without thinking, "That's not jade!"

Contact

If you need to contact me for any reason—to point out an error, to suggest a resource, or to ask for a bulk discount on copies of the book for a class, for example—you can get me on: mike@csidemedia.com.

There's a website for this book, where I'll announce any future books I write along similar lines, and publish additional material that will eventually be incorporated into future editions. That's at http://csidemedia.com/wellpresentedms.

If this book has been helpful to you, please spread the word, and consider leaving a review on the site where you bought it, or at a book review site such as Goodreads. Thanks!